India India F

India India Feeling

*Those were the days that were:
a light-hearted nostalgia*

Vikas Dhawan

authors
UPFRONT

To Mom and Dad

* * *

Ruhaan – this is how daddy grew up

Contents

Preface

*W*hat does India *feel* like?

What does any country feel like?

For me, the answer lies in the memories of childhood, of growing up, of learning to find one's place in the adult world.

It lies in the TV programmes I watched as a child, activities I indulged in during summer vacations, street food I relished, sports I played, vehicles that my dad bought, experiences I had in school, music I listened to, books I read and interactions I had with friends and relatives.

It lies in the heat of summers, fog of winters, power cuts that shaped daily routines and aspirations of a middle-class family in India.

The book flows through just that – memories of growing up in India of the times gone by. India as seen and felt through the mind of my younger self, India of the 1980s (and extending at the two ends, into the 1970s and the 1990s).

The 1980s was a sombre decade politically in India. The country endured through the assassination of Prime Minister Indira Gandhi, rise of terrorism, and the tragic events related to the Indian Peace Keeping Force in Sri Lanka. The decade was like a struggling family, trying to keep afloat, despite all the challenges.

In between, the nation enjoyed some bright spots. How can we forget the 1983 Cricket World Cup win by Kapil Dev and his team, and Rakesh Sharma travelling to space in 1984 – the first Indian to do so.

This was the decade that weathered the storm to allow for a more optimistic tomorrow, of the next decade of the 1990s.

Nevertheless, the 1990s brought its own political upheavals, particularly at the start of the decade. These included the assassination of the former prime minister, Rajiv Gandhi, and student protests against the central government's policy of reservation in education and jobs for some disadvantaged sections of the society, as mandated by the Mandal Commission.

The 1990s ushered in a fresh era, owing to the economic liberalisation brought in by the finance minister at that time, Dr Manmohan Singh, in the Narasimha Rao government. Suddenly, citizens had a choice. There were many more TV channels, a larger variety of cars and a mass uptake of computers and mobile phones. That was the beginning of the rise and rise of the Indian middle class.

You'll see the changes during that period as you move through the chapters in this book. Each chapter covers a particular aspect related to India during my growing up years – summer vacation, street food, cricket and others. The chapters can be read as standalone units, without dependence on each other. You may come across a slight repetition across some chapters as I talk about my circumstances in a different context in each chapter. Most chapters start with my childhood and end with the completion of my journey as a student – as a tax-free, carefree individual of society.

This book ends with a quiz to test your memory of advertisements that were shown on Indian television during the 1980s and the 1990s.

To those who are not familiar with the environments and objects covered in the book, I have added some explanation to help understand the context, hopefully without affecting the flow of reading. Translation of non-English words is provided when they first occur in the book. You will find a glossary of non-English words at the end of the book. Once you have finished reading the chapters, I will show you a few photographs, which I am sure you will enjoy.

The book is titled along the lines of the common practice of speaking certain words twice in a sentence in Hindi and other Indian languages. For instance, *dheere dheere chalna* (walking slowly; *dheere* = slow, *chalna* = walking), *bolte bolte chup ho jaana* (to stop talking mid-sentence), *halka halka yaad aana* (to remember vaguely).

I have used snippets from my growing up years to bring to life various aspects that constitute my 'India India' feeling. They are a recollection of my thoughts and memories and therefore may not link perfectly to one other. I wouldn't want to impose too much structure on them. Let memories enjoy the randomness that defines them.

I hope you will enjoy reading this book and get a glimpse of India of the yesteryears, quaint and charming, but at the doorstep of the new world. I also hope that some of you may relive your memories of those times, or your childhood, and in doing so find a reason to step back, pause and smile.

1.

Family on Scooter

*A*spirational, doubtful yet determined, on the cusp between tradition and something beyond tradition but not yet modern. And carrying on despite all odds, on a scooter. This was the rising Indian middle class in the 1980s.

In my mind, no image depicts this Indian family better than a young family on a scooter. The whole family. The ideal family size in those days was a pack of four – mom, dad and two children. This family employed other travel options too and went on to buy bikes and cars as the kids grew up and started using some of the money they had worked hard to save. But none carried the flag of ambition more than the family venturing out in the world on their scooter.

It was not easy to buy a scooter back then. You had to book well in advance. Some foreign-made scooters took up to 10 years to arrive at your doorstep. Imagine that. No wonder people would book a few scooters in their name and sell them in the black market.

Dad's first scooter was Vijay Super which he bought in 1978. The other main choices in those days were Lambretta, Bajaj Chetak and Bajaj Priya. I was rather young then and do not remember much of our Vijay Super. However, I do remember the Chetak that dad bought in 1982. By that time aspiration had found its innovation.

Foreign currency was in short supply in the country. So, if you paid in US dollars you could get your scooter sooner, in 6 months. *Jugaad*, as some would call it – the undying Indian spirit to find a solution whatever be the situation, be it a frugal, local innovation, or a hack!

However, the Indian middle class hit another bump on the road. How do you get foreign currency? In those days it was not common to emigrate to foreign lands. Few had the resources, need or exposure to do that, at least among the common folk. Dad somehow managed to find a friend who had a relative living in the US.

Dad gave Rs 12,000 to his friend, and the relative gave dad a cheque in US dollars. One US dollar was around Rs 10 at that time (nowadays it's about Rs 75). The American currency brought us our new scooter, Bajaj Chetak, grey, PBC 9752. The number is etched in my memory as this scooter was to become our companion for many years to come.

Now that you have your scooter, where do you park it? The scooter could not be parked overnight in the street where you lived as it was a precious, expensive asset. It had to be kept inside the house. But the entrance to our ancestral home in Ferozepur city (in the state of Punjab) was steep. It had 4 or 5 steps, along with a ramp. Dad had to push the scooter up the ramp every evening to keep it inside the house and roll it down every morning.

At times dad would park it at our neighbour's house because their front door was not as steep. However, it's not easy to inconvenience neighbours every day. Knowing dad, he would have hated asking a neighbour for an *ehsaan* (favour).

Dad was a happy man when he built his own house and we moved in. I was 11 at that time. He told us how delighted he was that he could simply drive the scooter through the main gate. No more pushing uphill or asking for a favour from neighbours. Small things bring us joy.

In those days, Ferozepur had an old-world charm. Horse-driven carts (tonga or *taanga* as they were called) were a common mode of transport, especially for school-going children. I vaguely remember sitting in a tonga with my sister (who is nearly two years older to me) as I left for my first day at school. I cried. So did mom. When I came back home that day, I told mom, "*Main taange wich no pya si*" (I cried in the tonga).

Routine takes over emotions. It was boarding the tonga to school every morning for us. The tonga stopped at various points in the city to collect children. The place where my sister and I boarded it was about a 3-minute walk from our house. It wasn't far. Yet, it seemed rather distant to me at that time.

Either mom or dad would accompany us to the tonga. If we were getting late, dad would drop us at the tonga-stop on our scooter. If we were way behind time, the tonga would leave without us. Its next stop was Gupta Madam's house. If we were on scooter, we rode the extra two minutes to that stop. Otherwise, we had to run through the market to reach that stop. If we had missed that stop and Gupta Madam was gone, then it was final. Dad had to take us all the way to school on scooter.

Pulling a tonga wouldn't have been easy on our horse. I hope my light weight helped the horse somewhat. It certainly helped in balancing the tonga. If the weight was not evenly distributed between the back and front of the tonga, the *taange waale* uncle who drove the tonga, and whom we called Tayaji (literal: uncle, father's elder brother), would make me move my seat to fine-tune the balance.

Tonga rides to the school used to be joyful, I have to say. As much as going to school can be. The tucc, tucc, tucc of horseshoe, the light breeze and not having to worry about income tax or electricity bills.

But tonga journeys were dangerous at times. There was a railway bridge on our way to school that connected the city to the army cantonment. It was en route to the Hussainiwala border between India and Pakistan. During the 1971 war, Pakistani aeroplanes targeted the bridge due to its strategic location. Fortunately, the bombs missed the bridge and hit the nearby railway lines instead.

Horses that pulled tongas were made to run as they climbed the bridge. Normally they managed it. Except, one day when our school tonga was about to reach the highest point of the bridge, our horse couldn't pull. The tonga started sliding backwards.

We were screaming. Our horse was scared and frantically trying to pull forward. The horse probably knew that lives of young children were at stake. It was possibly the smoke from the train passing underneath the bridge that affected our horse.

I had read the story of Black Beauty, the horse in the famous novel written by Anna Sewell, in my English class a few days before the incident. Black Beauty was scared of smoke puffing out of trains. I thought the same had happened to our horse.

Or perhaps the weight was too much for our poor horse. In that moment of panic, Tayaji asked a few of us to get down immediately. That helped. It may have been that the weight was not evenly distributed. The horse pulled it through and we reached school safely. I wish I could remember the name of our horse. It was a good horse.

There was another such incident on our tonga. We were about to reach the school when our horse got startled by something. It stopped immediately and raised its front feet in the air. We couldn't figure out what had happened. It felt like someone had applied emergency brakes. We all ended up tilting backwards. One student was sitting close to a wheel of the tonga. When the tonga stopped abruptly, his forehead was about to hit the wheel.

Those were big, strong, wooden wheels. Fortunately, another student, Sachin, who was sitting next to him, had the presence of mind to put his feet in between. So, this student's forehead hit Sachin's shoe instead of the wheel. Who knew what damage the wheel would have done. Well done, Sachin.

One day mom and dad came to our school. They met my sister and me, gave us hugs and kisses and left. It felt different. Why would they come to school like that? Why have tears in their eyes? When we left the school that day in our tonga we got to know that another tonga from our school had met with an accident that morning.

The tonga was passing underneath an old building and part of the building fell. Children sitting in the tonga were hit with bricks. So was the horse. The injured horse tried to pull but was killed, hit by sharp glass. The tonga driver survived with a glass injury in his eye. The children were taken to the hospital. Unfortunately, some of them did not survive.

The news spread in the city and someone alerted my mom. She didn't know which tonga had been hit, just that it was a tonga carrying students of our school. Dad was at work and could not be contacted immediately. So, mom went to the hospital by herself. She couldn't find us among the injured children. Then she saw a tall and thin-looking boy like me lying on the bed, dead. The worst fears. I dread to think how she must have felt. I dread to think of the parents whose son was lying on that bed. No parent should have to see such a day.

When we were a little older it was time to go to school on a bicycle. My bicycle arrived earlier than my sister's. We went to Ferozepur cantonment with dad to buy it as the city did not have an Atlas shop, a popular brand at that time. It was a silver-grey bicycle.

Dad started taking us to the municipal park to teach us how to ride it. He held the saddle from the back to balance the cycle as we paddled away. I didn't get to cycle to school for about a year, though. Our school was a bit of a distance from our house. Mom and dad did not want to risk sending me on a bicycle on busy roads. Perhaps they were extra cautious due to a tragic incident in our family at that time. My *bhuaji* (dad's sister) had lost her husband at a young age in a road accident, travelling on scooter.

My parents became more open to the idea of us cycling to school when we moved into our new house. It was closer to school. My sister was also given a new bicycle. It was a green Avon bicycle. Time to pedal to school. I enjoyed cycling to school. It gave me independence. I could go somewhere, on my own. I was in the driving seat.

My sister and I were pedalling home one afternoon after school. We were on the railway bridge close to our school. She was a few steps ahead. A bus came from behind and overtook us. We had to quickly steer our bicycles and were close to the railing of the bridge. My sister's bicycle somehow got stuck to the bus. Its handle got entangled in a metal bar at the rear of the bus.

She fell along with her bicycle and was being dragged by the bus. She was screaming. The bus was going downhill at speed. I thought she was going to die. I was there on my bicycle, dazed, helpless, watching her being dragged away. I doubt if the bus driver or any passenger could see what was going on. Then a miracle happened.

Her bicycle got disentangled from the bus on its own. The bus went off. She was left with her bicycle at the end of the bridge. People rushed to help. I cried. She got away with a few bruises. There must have been some god on the bridge that day, perhaps travelling on the bus.

Rickshaws were another common mode of transport for school. During my primary years, which I attended at Dasmesh Public School in Faridkot city (Punjab), my sister and I, and several other children from our neighbourhood, went to school on a rickshaw. We made 2 or 3 stops on the way to pick up other children. This included my cousin, daughter of my Mamaji (maternal uncle; mom's brother), who is a year younger to me. I made sure that her bag was stowed away and that she got a proper seat. Some are born responsible (others just claim it while writing).

Karnail Uncle pulled our rickshaw. I don't know how he managed to pull 8 or 10 youngsters and their school bags. He was an old, frail man with a white beard and wore a turban. Mom and dad would give Karnail Uncle cloth for a new turban at Diwali.

In addition to the main, upholstered seat, the rickshaw was fitted with an additional wooden seat in the front and a wooden slab at the back. Children sitting everywhere. If the rickshaw was over capacity, Karnail Uncle would adjust one child on the crossbar.

When teenage arrives, it brings along the need for speed. Rickshaws or bicycles won't do anymore. So, I started to learn how to drive a scooter. I was 15 years old at that time. Underage driving was common back then, and yes, it was illegal! Dad taught me how to drive. He rode pillion and guided me. The trickiest part was changing gears and learning to release the clutch slowly, and synchronising it with the accelerator (or 'race' as it is commonly called in many parts of India).

It was around this time that my sister started to prepare for medical college entrance exams; she had reached class 11. Dad bought her a moped (or 'scooterie' as it was also known) so that it was easier for her to attend a number of private tuitions – physics, chemistry and biology to be precise.

Our moped was a blue Panther model, having a PB 04 series number. Petrol was Rs 12 at that time and State-run Doordarshan was the sole TV channel.

We moved to Chandigarh due to dad's work. I started disliking our moped. It was acceptable in Punjab but not sleek and stylish for a modern city like Chandigarh. At least that's what I thought at that time. I was in class 11, 17 years of age and there were women folk around. What do you expect?

The helmet-wearing etiquette among young men in Chandigarh at the time was not to wear one. Helmets were carried along instead and as soon as a traffic cop, or *mama* (uncle) as they were lovingly called, was spotted, helmets would be put on. I also embraced the etiquette.

In the epic Mahabharat, we are told that Abhimanyu knew how to enter a *chakkarvyuh* (a military formation in the shape of a labyrinth) in a battle, but not how to exit one. He lost his life as a result. While I cannot claim that level of greatness, I too learnt how to carry a helmet with me but not how to wear it swiftly when traffic police were around. That resulted in my first *challan* (traffic ticket).

I never drove a two-wheeler without a helmet after that day. I still have nightmares where I am driving a scooter, realising midway that I am not wearing a helmet. Don't do it. Some of you may remember the advertisement on Doordarshan broadcast for public benefit (*jann hit mein jaari*). It showed a hammer falling on a coconut, without a helmet, and breaking it. The tagline: "*Marzi hai aapki, aakhir sir hai aapka*" (It is your choice, it is your head after all).

While we are on nightmares, another dream I often get is that my exams are starting after a couple of days and I haven't prepared anything. Or that the exam timetable was different from what I had thought it to be. Which meant I had prepared for the wrong subject and the exam was the next day. Worst nightmare for a student.

When I joined college, I was given our scooter to commute. At times, you had to tilt it towards you to start it. The scooter remained my partner on wheels through the college days. When you are in college, your scooter is not just your companion, it is that of your friends as well. Why would you drive a scooter with two passengers when it could fit in three?

Pushappreet, Gora and I would ride together on my scooter to our college. Triple riding (or 'triplee') was not allowed. You had to take inner roads where the likelihood of being caught was relatively low. Or the passenger at the very back had to remain in a ready state to jump off the scooter as soon as traffic police were spotted. Every day was an adventure.

Then came the day when we decided to buy a car. The family on scooter was not possible anymore. The family on scooter-plus-moped was not ideal either, especially where long distances were involved. And then there was status to be taken into account. Everyone we knew in Chandigarh had a car. It was decided that we should buy a second-hand car first, to learn how to drive and to save some money at that point.

Dad and I started scanning through the *Tribune* classifieds for second-hand cars. We also went to car bazaars, which were held at weekends. We couldn't find anything suitable, anywhere.

One of dad's cousins lived in Chandigarh. They ran a property management agency. They found out that we were looking for a car. And it so happened that they were looking to sell theirs. We paid Rs 1.35 lakh to buy a Maruti 800, white, CH01A 8823. Which other car, if not Maruti 800 in those days?

The car was left at our doorstep. There was one problem though. Neither dad nor I knew how to drive. So, we put a cover on it and it stayed there for some time.

Dad took lessons from a driving school. Then he taught me. I was in class 12, had celebrated my eighteenth birthday, so it was all legal this time. I picked up driving in a couple of days. Perhaps because as a child I used to observe my eldest Mamaji drive. I would watch keenly how he used the accelerator, clutch and brake. Or perhaps it was because of my naturally evolved synaptic connections. I think I drive well. Not sure why none of my passengers concur.

The car gave us problems from the word go. Dad and I could be found in the mornings pushing the car through our street. We spent uncountable weekends getting it repaired. We became regular customers at car garages and started receiving discounts. Dad became friends with car mechanics and had useful car-related conversations with them. Not me. Talking was never my thing. I just sat there with my air of assumed, self-proclaimed superiority, watching the world as it went on with its routine.

Shayad unka aakhri ho yeh sitam,
Har sitam yeh soch kar hum seh gaye.

(Thinking that it might be their last injustice [in love], I kept on bearing every pain afflicted by them.)

These lines, sung by Salma Agha in the movie *Nikaah* (1982), sums up our experience of our first car. We thought every repair was the last one. But every time it managed to teach us the famous concept of Vedic mathematics, *ekadhiken purvena* – one more than the previous one.

You tell me if I am wrong. This one time my friends in college decided to go to Timber Trail, which is in Parwanoo in the state of Himachal Pradesh. Not far from Chandigarh. It is a famous tourist attraction where people take a cable car ride surrounded by the hills of Shivalik. Heights was never my idea of fun. But when friends have decided, friends have decided. They also decided that we should go in my car (well, dad's, technically speaking).

Little did they know what they were getting into, literally. Even I did not expect any misdemeanour from the car that day. It was working fine. And it was just 35 kilometres. Granted, we were going to the mountains. But it was only at the foothills. We were merely asking you to drive us to Parwanoo, not all the way to Shimla.

There is a famous shop at the corner of the main road close to the Timber Trail where you can buy fruit juice, made from fresh apples and other fruit produced in Himachal Pradesh. Our car broke down in front of the shop. There was smoke coming out of the bonnet. It was the first time I had seen our car smoke unabashedly in front of me.

Neeraj was the more worldly-wise in our group. He opened the bonnet. After which his wisdom ran out. He opened the lid of the coolant reservoir and out came hot liquid and splashed over his face.

His fault of course. It was his decision not to move his face away when opening the lid. He was wearing glasses, so his eyes were safe. But there was hot, green liquid on his face. We had a water bottle (I always travelled well prepared) and he quickly washed his face. Don't worry, he was fine in the end.

We pushed the car to Timber Trail and spent a couple of hours there, hoping that the car would cool down. And it did. It started working when we were to drive back home. But the deal it struck was: *I will run and let you steer me, but won't allow my headlights to switch on. Are we all OK with that? Yes?*

We accepted the deal. Only that it was late in the evening and dark. What do you do now?

Jugaad. I had a torch in the car (told you, well prepared). Goldy, who was sitting next to me in the front, lowered the window glass and held the torch out throughout the journey. We thought this would at least make us visible to other vehicles on the road. This was the youth of India in that car that day, carrying the torch of innovation.

How sensible was our idea? Who knew, who cared. It was fun, made all the more worthwhile with Neeraj muttering all the way back home, "*Yaar, eh coolant hot kidan ho gya?*" (How could a coolant turn hot?) It was supposed to have remained cool!

Finally, we sold the car. We used it, or it used us, for 5 years. The anti-incumbency was a powerful factor. So, we bought a brand-new Hyundai Santro. I remember the smell of the fresh, new car. That was a good car. It was to stay in our family for the next 10 years. It didn't give us much trouble. But it did give me terrible heartbreak on the first day.

When we drove the car back home after purchasing it, it made considerable noise. It was frustrating. It was painful. No relief from car troubles, I wondered. We went back to the car dealer. They took a test drive and said that it was absolutely fine.

It turned out that I was putting it into the third gear when I was intending the fifth gear. Now, before you give your judgement, it wasn't my fault. It was the first time I was driving a 5-gear car. Our previous car had four gears. So I couldn't figure out the correct gear position. Told you, not my fault after all.

I wasn't a motorbike type. I tried it a couple of times. Neeraj had a Suzuki Shogun and Mohit had a Royal Enfield Bullet (lovingly called 'Bullt' in that part of the world). I tried both. They were good. Hero Honda bikes were also attractive, or perhaps I liked their advertisement tagline – "Fill it, shut it, forget it". However, I chose my family scooter, my Bajaj Chetak, to be my companion – tilt it, start it, forget it.

2.

School Life

*W*hen I was young, I thought every child went to school. How wrong I was. There are millions of children who are unable to attend school. I now realise how lucky I was. I dedicate this chapter to every child who has not been fortunate enough to go to school.

The pre-school I went to in Ferozepur in Punjab was called 'Sharma's School'. It was less than 5 minutes' walk from our house. I have faint memories of the school – holding mom's hand while walking to the school, the narrow staircase that led into the premises, getting sweet candies, small, round, white ones contained in a small cardboard box. Mom used to leave the candies with the teacher in case I felt unsettled.

Dad worked at State Bank of India and by the time I completed my nursery, dad was transferred to Faridkot, a city not far from Ferozepur. I was admitted to Dasmesh Public School in LKG (Lower Kindergarten). That is where I also did my UKG (Upper Kindergarten) and class 1. I have little memory of that time, except that there was a separate playground for us young 'uns, with swings and see-saws.

After 3 years dad was transferred back to Ferozepur. It was time to find our next school. I had finished class 1 and my sister had finished class 3. Mom and dad wanted to give us the best schooling, perhaps like all middle-class parents at that time. So, it was decided that we would apply to St. Joseph's Convent School, which was well-known in the region.

The academic year had just started. We were asked to appear for an admission test. On the day of the test, we went to the school on dad's scooter; mom sitting at the back with me, and my sister standing at the front. We were given the test and apparently both of us did well.

The school principal said that both of us could jump a class each. The fact that both of us were tall also seemed to have contributed to that decision, so we were told. I was promoted straight to class 3 instead of class 2 and my sister jumped one class to class 5.

Mom told us later that en route to school that day she was praying all the time and repeating this couplet from Hanuman Chalisa − *Sankat te hanuman churrave, mann karam bachan dhyan jo laave* (Lord Hanuman protects and removes obstacles of those who remember him with sincerity). She attributed our admission to the prayer. Who can ever tell? The poet Mirza Ghalib (1797–1869) had a different way of saying this.

Dekhiye paate hain ushshaaq buton se kya faiz,
ik brahman ne kaha hai, ke yeh saal acha hai.

(Let's see what favours do lovers/disciples get from their beloved/deity, a soothsayer has told me this will be a good year for me.)

I fared well in my studies in class 3. So perhaps it was a good year for me after all. The trend in the school was that the top-performing girl and the top-performing boy in class were made 'monitors' in the next class. I was made the monitor in class 4, along with Tanya. For the next 3 years, both of us were to be appointed monitors of our class. However, being a monitor does not protect you from everything. Call of nature for one.

Once, I *had* to go. The shortest distance between where I was at that moment in time and space and where one could go when one had to go was the staff toilet in school. I went for it. The bolt inside the toilet was at the top of the door. Young little me, even though tall, could not reach the bolt. There was no time left to go anywhere else. So I just sat down.

Then the worst that could happen, happened.

The door opened. There was light at the doorstep. A furious figure appeared, and quickly disappeared. The door closed and I heard a voice, "Come outside and see me."

"Yes ma'am."

I went outside and couldn't see anyone. I could have just run away. But the moral dilemma stepped in. So, I went looking and found the teacher sitting on a chair alongside another teacher.

"Shame on you."

"Sorry, ma'am."

"Do you not know that this is the staff toilet?"

"Sorry, ma'am."

"How long have you been here?"

"From class 3 ma'am."

"Which 3rd?"

"3B, ma'am."

And then something that had never happened to me before in school happened. It came with a sound, a pain that I had never experienced. I got a slap, a tight one, on my innocent little cheek. There was sobbing involved, I can tell you that.

"Go back to your class and don't ever use the staff toilet again."

I learnt two lessons that day. One, do not take shortcuts in life and second, do not sit on someone else's throne.

The slap was perhaps the first reminder that mom and dad could not protect me everywhere and that I wasn't 'unslappable'. I did eke out a small victory in all this, I thought. The teacher asked me how long had I been studying at the school and then which section.

I gave the correct answer – 3B. But I was not in class 3 *anymore*. She did not ask me the right question, my current class. I was in class 4. And not 4B but 4A. Which meant that she thought I was in 3B. So, she wouldn't be able to find me. She didn't ask my name either. I was safe, I thought.

I was safe. She didn't come hounding for the juvenile who used her toilet. But she did leave me scarred for life. Since that day I have never been able to use a toilet without checking the door lock twice or thrice. No peace even in the toilet for some.

There was another childhood experience that led to a habit that continues to date. I was at home and was getting ready to go out. As I put on my shoes, I felt something soft moving inside one of my shoes.

I panicked, removed the shoe and flung it in the air. A big frog jumped out of it, looking at me as if I had done something wrong (*you were wearing the wrong size shoe, not me, my friend*). Terrible experience. I haven't been able to wear shoes since then without turning them upside down. Never, ever. I just can't.

On birthdays we were allowed to wear 'civil dress' instead of school uniform. That day, in the morning, the birthday girl or boy would stand in front of the class and everyone would sing 'Happy Birthday'. Then the birthday girl or boy would distribute sweets to all the students in their class and the class teacher. On my birthday in class 4, mom and dad bought me a big bag of sweets. I had plenty of sweets remaining after distributing two each to all my class fellows.

During the lunch break, I carried the bag to the playground.

One of my class fellows wished me again, so I gave him two extra sweets. Which meant he now had 4 sweets of me. Hmm. I noticed that he was talking to other students, not from our class; all these children started wishing me one by one. I now had to give sweets to them, which I did.

I reasoned that my class fellow was telling them that this fella is giving away all his sweets, you just need to say happy birthday to him. He was being extra smart. That upset me. It was my birthday, my sweets, my large-heartedness.

He now sent another kid to me, who came and wished me. I said thank you. He waited. He again said happy birthday. I again said thank you. He waited, so did I, and then he left, without any sweets. I held my ground. This was the right thing to do, was it not?

The laws of karma thought otherwise, it seems. Diwali that year brought a box of *gulab jamuns* from a colleague of dad. If you haven't tried them, they are sweet fried dough balls, soaked in rose-flavoured sticky syrup, usually served warm. I ate almost half the box, 12 gulab jamuns, and that too cold, in a day. As a result, I couldn't speak at all for the next 15 days. I lost my voice. I could hardly swallow anything.

Doctors said that I would need to get my tonsils operated upon. However, dad was not keen to go ahead. Someone in our family had a nerve damaged by mistake during a similar operation, losing an eye as a result.

It must have been a difficult decision for my parents. The surgery was not done and I was given medicines instead. I got better after a few days. But my voice changed after that. Those gulab jamuns may have cost the world the voice of another Kishore Kumar or Manna Dey. Who knows.

I enjoyed attending the school assembly that took place every morning. There would be neat queues of students from every class moving towards the assembly ground. I can recall a couple of prayers that we sang during assembly.

- *Tumhi ho mata pita tumhi ho, tumhi ho bandhu sakha tumhi ho* (You are my heavenly mother, my divine father, you are my real kinsman, my true friend).
- *Tere sanmukh sheesh jhukha dein hum baalak nadaan* (We, your innocent children, bow our heads to you with reverence).
- *Itni shakti humein dena daata, mann ka vishwaas kamzor ho na* (O Lord, give us strength so that our trust, our belief, our resolve does not weaken).

Then the national anthem was sung.

On Saturdays, we would wear fleet shoes (running shoes). That day, after assembly, we would have the school parade. We marched left, right, left on the beats of drums – a bass drum and a snare drum. I would imagine myself playing the drums. But unfortunately, I never got a chance to play the drums at the school assembly.

I did however play beats on my desk in class using pens and pencils, adding snare effect using a foot ruler that was elevated at one end by keeping a pencil sharpener underneath.

Class 5 was happening. It was the start of upper primary schooling. I started the second decade of my life. We could choose an additional language at school, apart from English. I started learning Punjabi. The speaking part was never a problem as it was my first language. However, writing in Gurmukhi (the script used for writing Punjabi in India) was a new experience.

It's a shame that regional languages are not given as much emphasis as English in schools in India, especially in the urban areas. The result is that I find it easier to write using the English alphabet instead of Punjabi or Hindi. I am sure there are millions, like me, who have experienced the same.

There was an essay in our Punjabi book on the value of mother tongue. It was written by the famous Bollywood actor Balraj Sahni, who also made a remarkable contribution to Punjabi literature. I believe the essay was an extract from his book *Mera Rusi Safarnama*, a travelogue, where he talks about his tour to the erstwhile Soviet Union in 1969.

He narrates a folktale of a Russian mother who covers her face with a veil when she learns that her son does not use his mother tongue anymore (which, according to the local customs, meant that she considered him dead, and hence the veil). I cannot claim that I remember the exact story after all these years, but the theme of the story was *ma boli* (mother tongue), and the role we should be playing in respecting it, in preserving it.

Our class prepared a dance for the school annual function that year and I also took part in it. It was a traditional dance from Nagaland I believe. There was a girl and a boy pairing and we practised at lunch breaks. I was a natural of course.

At the annual day, I wore a traditional dress – well, sort of. Waist down it was made of peepul tree leaves sewn together which were then clipped on my waist.

We were standing behind the stage, and just one act before ours, I thought that my costume wasn't holding up well. So, I asked a *didi* – one of the senior girls – from the organising committee to help me out. A few minutes before our performance, my dress was unfastened and clipped back again with safety pins. Our dance began.

Roombak jhumba dagariya dole,
Paakkar chhaakar dagariya dole,
Ya sayyiaan ingo nee…

*Apologies if the lyrics are not correct. This is what I could remember.
I could not find the song online as well to verify. If you do know the
correct lyrics, I would love to hear from you.*

As I was busy doing gyrations on stage, my leafy dress started
coming off. It became loose and fell off from one side. I was
shattered. What a nightmare, I thought. Thank goodness for
the shorts I was wearing underneath the costume. I was later
informed that the video recording also captured my wardrobe
malfunction. At least I made the audience laugh.

Can you recall the names of your schoolmates? How about
the first friend you had in school? Names of several of my class
fellows over the years are coming to mind. Nikunj became my
'best friend'. Amit, Harpreet, Sachin, Sarabjeet, Nidhi, Tina,
Ashwin, Alka, Pooja, Preeti, Raman, Tanisha, Manu and more.
I wonder what all of them are up to in life nowadays.

It was not easy being the class monitor. You had to balance
your responsibility and your friendships. Youngsters can turn
unruly if there is no teacher in a classroom. Perhaps, this
exemplifies the line of thought that morality exists or augments
in society because of policing, real or perceived, by State or
fellow human beings or divine power.

Cruel thing, logic. It doesn't always work in your favour.
Once I was standing in front of my class, minding it because
there was no teacher in class. I was just doing my duty when
came barging a teacher and slapped me.

"Why are you not on your seat?"

There was pin-drop silence. It was just the tears that
rolled. She had hit me. She had hit my ego. I have never been
able to accept unfairness. But I didn't have it in me to utter
a word.

A girl in my class then said, "Ma'am, he is the monitor."

Why did you hit me, ma'am? Did you not know that I was the monitor? Were you new to the school? You were? Oh.

I was in class 6 when the Mandal Commission happened. Students across the country were protesting against the central government policy of reservation in education and jobs for historically disadvantaged sections of the society. Schools and colleges throughout the country were shut down in protest.

The college-going boys and girls would come to our school to get it closed for the day. They normally came in the period after lunch. Perhaps they started in the morning going from one school to the next before reaching our school in the afternoon.

We would get pretty excited to see them because we knew what it meant. The school would close for the day after they arrived. This happened for several days. A school holiday was a fabulous gift for us. Little did we realise how terrible the whole situation was. Several young students committed suicide by setting themselves on fire in protest against the government policy. It was tragic.

I had finished my class 7 and my sister class 9. It was time for us to move. Dad was transferred to Faridkot again. We were back in our previous school – Dasmesh Public School. It was known to be one of the best schools in the region. And a completely different one for us. We moved from a convent-run school to a school that followed Sikh traditions.

We had an exceptional school principal in Mr Gurcharan Singh. He was always well-dressed and wore a tie and turban of the same colour. He was MA in English and often taught us the correct pronunciation of English words such as sabotage – *sab-oh-thaaaj*, as he would say and make us repeat many times.

Principal Sir wanted that the students should be well-versed in English and we were asked to speak in English with each other. Two 'prefects' were chosen from each class who would enforce this directive. I was selected as one of the prefects in my class. A boost to my ego. I was somebody in this school, after all, I thought. Little did I realise how challenging it was going to be.

Every prefect was given a card, which they were to hand over to anyone not speaking in English in their class. This student would pass the card ahead to anyone who defaulted speaking in English. At the end of the day, the prefect had to collect a fine from everyone who had the card that day. The fine was 50 paisa for the first offence in a day by a student. For further offences it doubled to Rs 1, then Rs 2, Rs 4 and so on.

Students paid their fines for one or two days. After that, they just stopped talking when I was around. And then they stopped talking to me at all, as you would expect. It is not easy for any student if your class fellows stop talking to you. But I carried on upholding my responsibility. I was the saviour of English, in the heart of tempestuous, rustic Punjab, in the 1980s.

One day I entered the den of a group of boys in my class who came from a nearby village. I handed over my speak-English-else-get-fined card to one of them and explained the fine. They all looked at me. They were tall, well-built guys, and I with my size 0 frame standing in front of them hanging by the faith in my card. I wondered what they were thinking. After all, I was their prefect, I reasoned.

"*Saade ton English bulwayega*" (He will make *us* speak in English), one of them scorned.

Yes, that was the whole point, I thought.

In my mind, I was calculating the money I would get from all of them. All of a sudden, I found my English-speaking card, my identity, my id, ego and super-ego combined in one, flying towards me.

"*Aa lai aapna card, te kar lai jo karna*" (Take your card and do whatever you can do to us).

This was followed by a round of expletives. Should I hand the card back, I thought, because the expletives were still not in English.

I measured the benefits against the risk involved and decided that the risk was rather high. Bones, once broken, are difficult to put together. English will survive, with or without me.

The English prefect scheme was suspended after some time. I could make friends again. Johnny and Monu became close friends. There was Puneet who lived next door and became a good friend, along with Sukhija who was an intellectual, humble guy. I think back on cycling home from school during hot summer afternoons along with my friends, discussing politics and how we would change the world. We were 15.

Our school was the first one in the region to get computers for students. It was the late 1980s and these were the good old BBC computers. The characters appeared in green on the computer screen. The CPU had a 5 1/4-inch floppy drive.

We were given one floppy disk each. We were asked to keep floppy disks in the fridge at home because they could go kaput due to hot weather. We had to remove our shoes outside the computer room. No, not out of respect but to avoid taking any dirt inside and risk damaging the computers or floppy disks.

We loved our weekly computer class because, apart from the excitement of using the machines, we could sit in an air-conditioned room which was a luxury in those days.

The first computer programme I wrote was to join two dots using their x and y coordinates. I also remember creating a car by joining several dots and circles. It was amazing. I could create something on my own, and see it take shape immediately in front of my eyes. Wasn't that fantastic.

We had some incredible teachers. We respected them, feared them, admired them. To us, they were the embodiment of the real, adult world out there.

Manjit Ma'am, our English teacher, Kochhar Ma'am our social studies teacher, Kashyapp Sir our maths teacher. Kochhar Ma'am had taught in my previous school, the convent school. Therefore, I was delighted to see her again. Ranjit Ma'am, our Punjabi teacher was strict and serious and therefore amusing to us teenagers.

Manjit Ma'am gave us a tip which I carry with me till date – using 'did' with past tense in a sentence is like putting *bindi* on your dad's forehead. You never do it. The bindi is meant to adorn your mom's face, not your dad's.

One of our teachers had a small cane with him to punish students. He believed in hitting students to discipline them. He even gave a name to his cane – Maulabaksh (literally meaning someone spared or purified of sins by one's master or God). This is affection for you.

Our music teacher, Mehta Sir, turned out to be a distant relative. I started taking private lessons in guitar at his home. He had a Hawaiian guitar. I went for lessons for a few days till my interest waned. String instruments were not my thing. I was interested in percussion. So, I started looking for opportunities to play the drums.

We had a drum kit at our school. But it was locked in a room. I managed to get its key from Mehta Sir a couple of times to practice during lunch breaks. But that didn't carry on for long as I was not comfortable asking for the key again and again.

The daily assembly in the school was held in the ground which was encircled by all the classrooms. There was a big stage made of concrete. Students from all the classes would stand around the stage in queues. It seemed like a daily chore then but I miss that now.

Principal Sir would give us a speech sometimes, either on English language or ethics in life or purpose of schooling. We sang prayers from Gurbani – hymns and other compositions contained in the Guru Granth Sahib, the most revered scripture in Sikhism. The prayer I cherish the most was this one composed by Shri Guru Gobind Singh (the tenth Sikh guru):

Deh shiva var mohe hain, shubh karman te kabhoon na daroon

(O Lord bless me so that I may never be afraid to do good deeds)

Inspiring lyrics, mesmerising sound of harmonium, hundreds of students singing together in an open ground. It was pure gold.

We had a large playground in the school, which was flanked by the boy's hostel and accommodation for teachers on one side and an open field on the other side. There was a huge wind turbine in the field to draw up water. Having a wind turbine in those days, and that too in a school was unparalleled. Principal Sir was a visionary, no doubt.

There are some experiences which you are not meant to have as a child. Experiences that shake your innocent view of the world. Experiences that leave scars on young minds.

One day we heard the tragic news that one of our teachers had committed suicide. Perhaps due to some issues in his personal life. He jumped in front of a moving train, not far from the railway crossing close to our school. We used to pass the railway crossing every day. I could never look at the crossing with the same fondness again. How much suffering he must have endured to take that step. His children studied at our school. How much they must have suffered.

This is not the kind of news you expect to hear about your teachers at that age. You are not prepared for that. For a child, teachers, parents and other adults in the family are infallible.

They are the rocks, ever-present for you to hold on to. But you can never tell what's going on inside someone's mind. A little kindness towards others, and self, could possibly go a long way in alleviating pain in the world we live in, for us and for the future generations.

Conflicts affect children the most, be it personal, social or political. Those were the days when the state of Punjab, the beautiful, hearty Punjab, was going through the dark phase of militancy. Violent incidents and killings were frequent. One of my class friends was going on a train journey with his family at night. Armed men stopped the train midway and fired from outside on passengers through the open windows. Many lives were lost.

My friend's younger brother got hit by a bullet on his shoulder. My friend later described to me how they used a towel to press the wound, and how the towel got soaking wet. Fortunately, his brother survived. I kept on thinking what was the fault of my friend's brother. He was merely a 10-year-old child. He shouldn't have to go through that. I shouldn't have to think through that at school. I was there to learn.

Terror struck our school once. One day a couple of terrorists tried to force their way into the school while the classes were on. They were armed with guns. However, our gutsy peon managed to close the door. He somehow made sure that they could not enter the school and they fled. Our peon was an elderly man, wearing spectacles and a turban. Who knows how many lives that brave, old man saved that day.

Despite all this, life moved on. Which for us meant more studies, more essays and more exams.

When I was in class 10 things became hectic. The teachers, class fellows, parents, all gearing up for the end of the year board exams. People started attending private tuitions, there were revision classes at school and several mock tests were held including pre-board exams. The class 10 exam was the first external test in those days, the chance to finally see how you fared nationally in the CBSE (Central Board of Secondary Education) exams.

When we were about to finish class 10, Principal Sir came to our class and said that we would always carry the school with us. Because of the foundation that the school had laid for the life ahead. And because the class 10 CBSE certificate would mention the school's name along with the date of birth, which we would need as an identity proof wherever we would go next.

We were given a farewell from school. I was 16 at that time. The board exams happened. And there you go. The innocent, protected school life was over. Now the race to be somebody started.

3.

Newspaper: The Akhbaar

*D*uring my teenage years, I picked up from somewhere that news was an acronym for north, east, west and south. That was a revelation for me. I thought someone, somewhere, at some point in history, would have devised this word, thinking that I, on this day, need a word for something that could happen anywhere and come from any direction.

It could come from north or south, east or west. What about using the first letter of these words – NSEW? But this isn't easy on the tongue to pronounce. There needs to be a vowel in between N and S. What about NESW? Still not there. How about moving the S at the end, NEWS? Yes. Voila, the word was born to enlighten the world thereafter.

Only that this is not true. The word 'news' did not start its journey as an acronym for the four directions as is a common belief. It most likely comes from the word 'new', having origins in the French word *nouvelles*.

The main thing is that current information, printed on paper, has been termed as newspaper. I have loved it as my *akhbaar*.

Why is it called akhbaar? Now you are talking. The question did not strike me until now. Our acceptance of words as they are, and the world as it is, is perhaps an integral part of us becoming one with the society around us. More so for a newborn. Which perhaps is also the reason why babies are happy.

Until now no one told me why an akhbaar is called so. Thanks to Google, I can tell you that akhbaar has Arabic origins, and is a plural of *khabar* or news.

Google also tells me that in Hindi it is called *samacharpatra*. I will stick to how I have known it – akhbaar.

My earliest memory of the daily akhbaar is dad reading news to my grandad, whom we called Bauji (a word of address used in respect for father or grandfather or any other elderly man in a family). Dad and Bauji would sit in our open-air verandah in the centre of the house, with their chairs facing each other. This was done in the morning before dad went to work or sometimes in the evening.

Dad read the main headlines first, followed by details of important news or of those that Bauji would ask after. Bauji would nod, or at times give his comments to some stories, lamenting what politicians were up to. Dad would agree with Bauji's reflections. I would sit there watching this interlude between a father and a son. I was lucky to have grandparents around me when I was growing up. They leave you rich by being there.

The newspaper we bought at that time was *Punjab Kesari*, a Hindi daily. Bauji's photo was published in the newspaper frequently as the newspaper would publish details of donors to the '*shaheed parivar* fund' run by the newspaper. Literally speaking, the fund for martyr's families, it was meant to help families affected by terrorism in Punjab in the 1980s.

Newspapers were not used solely for reading. They were also used in shops as wrapping paper. Clothes were wrapped in newspapers and tied with a thread. Drinking glasses, china plates, mirrors, and other family bric-a-brac were wrapped in newspapers. Plastic bags were less common in those days, which was good for the environment.

If you were having street food – *chaat* (a spicy mix of fruit or boiled vegetables) or, *samosa*, you name it – they were likely to be served on a square piece of a newspaper. (If you insist, a samosa is a triangle-shaped fried pastry filled with potatoes and peas or other fillings. You knew that already, didn't you?)

My interest in newspapers started when I was about 17. I started spending more and more time going through newspapers. I wanted to read everything except my study books. Newspapers opened a world of possibilities for me. My daily diet became richer and richer in newsprint.

Entering college gave me more freedom. The pressure of studies was not as intense. I had more time to pursue my interests and made some good friends. Bhatnagar's dad worked in the *Tribune*, which has its headquarters in Chandigarh, the capital city for the states of Punjab and Haryana. It was the most admired newspaper in and around Chandigarh at that time and had a loyal readership. The newspaper was founded in 1881 in Lahore by Sardar Dyal Singh Majithia.

The *Tribune* occupies a large building in Chandigarh, next to what is known as the Tribune Chowk, a large roundabout covered by plants and flowers, now also surrounded by traffic lights to cope with the ever-growing traffic. Outside the *Tribune* office, there is a large electronic news ticker that displays the headlines and lights up at night.

I was lucky to visit the building from inside. Bhatnagar's dad showed us around the premises. I saw newspapers being churned out at fast speeds in the printing press. I had never seen such a huge machine in my life. It was majestic. I touched the newspapers, hot off the press. I could smell fresh ink. I witnessed with my own eyes how my newspaper was printed. That was a special moment for me.

How fantastic it is for the youngsters to visit manufacturing facilities and see how things are made. Schools have a role to play here in organising such trips. One such experience could give a spark of life-changing inspiration to a child, something that years and years of spoon-feeding in classrooms and regurgitation in exams might not.

When I would visit Bhatnagar's house, I watched his dad cut out articles of interest from newspapers (their family received a large number of newspapers daily, much to my envy). He used a foot ruler made of steel to cut the articles out. He would paste the articles on blank A4 papers and file them in plastic folders.

I knew I had to get a foot ruler exactly like that. You could also use a plastic foot ruler, but it is not as sharp as a metallic one and doesn't give that crisp sound when you tear a newspaper. Like Bhatnagar's dad, I also started pasting articles that I cut out on blank A4s and built an endearing collection.

Press has power. I realised that when Bhatnagar happened to have a scuffle with a group of boys at college. His dad got a whiff of it and drove to our college with a jeep-load of policemen. The college staff scrambled around to get the matter resolved quickly and amicably.

However, for common folk the power of the press gets delivered straight to their homes. The best time of my day was getting up in the morning and heading to our flat's balcony to pick up my newspaper. I preferred being woken up by the sound of newspaper dropping on our balcony. Why would one even want to wake up before it arrived?

The newspaper vendors were real experts. They would hold their bicycle with one hand, roll a newspaper, tie a thread around it and throw it with the other hand. This all happened in a second. I had never seen them miss their target balcony or throw it with such force that it broke any window glass.

They also had to make sure that they delivered newspapers to all the houses in their territory before 8 am. Anything later than that meant people like me would start becoming restless. The days when I did not find the newspaper on our balcony, even after searching behind all the flower pots, brought the pain of longing worse than Sufi saint Bulle Shah's longing for his guru.

Finding a different newspaper than my usual was almost equally bad, especially on Saturday and Sunday when weekend features were published. But none as bad as not finding any newspaper at all. When you need a newspaper, you need a newspaper.

When I didn't find one, I would pick up our scooter to search for our newspaper vendor. Or any other newspaper vendor in our neighbourhood. You could buy a newspaper from some vendors on the spot. But most of them had an exact number of newspapers that they had set out to deliver. So no newspaper for you over there. Bad luck.

My next port of call was a nearby stationery shop. Luck mattered even here. Sometimes they had the newspaper I wanted, sometimes they did not. What could you do? You made yourself leave the house in the morning. You were on the hunt now. You would head straight to the jungle, wouldn't you?

Which in this case was the ultimate place for buying newspapers, the Everest for those in search of newsprint, the main bus stand. It was in Sector 17 in Chandigarh, nearly 8 km away from our residence. The bus stand had paid parking. And you had to pay (no getting away by 'talking' to the parking attendant). The parking fee was three times the price of a newspaper. But that was never a deterrent.

When you bring a child to a toy shop, they will want to

buy all the toys. How could I leave with a single newspaper now that I was at the bus stand, looking at heaps of different newspapers? At least two or three newspapers had to be bought to justify my trek.

Bookstalls at bus stands do not just stock newspapers. They have magazines and books on offer. I was fortunate to have an insider view of bookstalls as one of my friends in college, Neeraj, owned bookstalls at the bus stand. Or his dad did.

Neeraj's dad had a humble beginning, reading out stories or poems to advertise the books he sold in trains. He gradually bought a permanent stall at the Chandigarh bus stand, and then a few more stalls which was no small feat given how expensive these stalls were. He later started a printing press, which is now run by Neeraj and his brothers. If you have less, you have more hunger to succeed.

But I was content with just buying newspapers and magazines at the stalls. There were plenty of magazines like *Competition Master* and *Competition Success Review (CSR)* to prepare for various competitive exams such as MBA, engineering, banking and the UPSC (Union Public Service Commission) that led to joining the government services.

I had already subscribed to the *CSR*, so a visit to the bus stand was a chance to buy *Competition Master*. And *India Today* for news and views. *Business Today* and *Sportsworld* were less frequent in my cart.

Another magazine that was added in my collection was *Businessworld*. It had been launched recently at that time. I received a one-year free subscription to the magazine along with the first internet connection I bought. The connection was provided by Satyam internet service.

The modems were dial-up at that time and made a cringing sound as if trying hard to connect you to the internet, mostly ending in a 'tick' sound which meant *sorry, couldn't connect, let me try again*. When they did connect, the speed was so slow that you could log onto a webpage, finish your meal and come back and the page would still be loading.

So as the irony would have it, the internet brought along the first news magazine that was delivered to my doorstep regularly. After the end of the free subscription for *Businessworld*, I happily paid to extend it for another year and another.

The best things in life are free, they say. Be it nature, watching a baby smile or experiencing inner peace. But there is something special when you get 'free gifts'. And what better way than to win some in newspaper and magazine competitions.

The first competition that I won was a general knowledge quiz in a magazine called *Suman Saurabh*. I was studying in school at that time and went on a visit to Mamaji's place who had subscribed to the magazine. I answered the current affairs quiz in the magazine and posted my responses.

There were three prizes – Rs 100, Rs 50 and Rs 25. I was delighted to read my name in the following issue. I had won Rs 25, on my own accord. I cut out the page with the quiz results as a memento and started a diary to note down my competition winnings.

I entered many competitions after that. Postcards were sought after in those days for competition entries. I bought them, the yellow ones, in bulk. TV serials also fuelled the use of postcards. Several TV programmes started quiz competitions, inviting entries on postcards. Millions of postcards were added to the system by people wanting to win prizes. I am not sure if the postal department would have been happy or upset about it.

I had to wait until I was in class 11 for my next win. It was in a TV programme on the business and share market called *Rajendra, a few rupees more*. Rajendra was perhaps the name of the anchor or the sponsor. They had a quiz question and declared several winners every week. The prize was an investment guide (written by Rajendra perhaps).

I did not need a book on financial advice – I was 17. I just wanted to win. And I did. When the names of winners rolled on our TV screen one week, I saw my dad's name roll past. You see one person was allowed one entry. So, I had made one entry in my name and another one in dad's name. However, dear friends, readers and fellow scribes, we never received that book. I waited and waited. I made an entry in my diary to keep a record of my winnings. But the book never arrived. Rajendra, you owe me a book, pal.

I won a few general knowledge quiz competitions and caption contests in the *Tribune* and *Chandigarh Newsline* (published by the Indian Express group). The *Tribune* also gave me the most tangible gifts I had won. The newspaper published competitions during the 1996 Cricket World Cup, which was held in the Indian subcontinent. They were giving away prizes every week. I won a briefcase. And another briefcase the next month.

These briefcases till date hold a mélange of my memories – all the diaries, stamps and coins I collected, and photographs, photo negatives, newspaper cuttings, and address books – the things that I held dear at that time. It is all in there. But perhaps the most cherished item of 'em all is the postcard that I received from Khushwant Singh (1915–2014).

I was a regular reader of his column – 'This Above All' – in the *Tribune*. He had a distinctive logo for his articles – him sitting in a bulb with a scroll of paper and a pen, along with some books and an inkpot. Another weekly column that he wrote, 'With malice towards one and all', was also well admired, along with his Hindi column '*Na kaahu se dosti na kaahu se bair*' (Friendship with none, hostility towards none).

His articles were a mixture of his views, which were forthright, jokes sent by readers to him and a poem or a couplet. I picked up interest in Mirza Ghalib after reading this *sher* (couplet) composed by the poet, featuring in 'This Above All':

Kahin mehkhaane ka darwaaza Ghalib aur kahaan waayiz,
Par itna jaante hain kal woh jaata tha ke hum nikle.

(A priest is poles apart from alcohol, but yesterday I saw him entering a pub/bar as I left.)

It is worth saying that the literal translation given here and elsewhere in the book is unlikely to bring home the deeper meaning of the couplets. The richness of poetry is in what is left unsaid.

Khushwant Singh would have explained Ghalib's sher better and with a bit more swag. He had a close, endearing relationship with alcohol. In one of his articles, he said that there was a proper method of drinking whisky. Every evening, he said, he would sit down before dinner, sprinkle some whisky around him and then pour it in a glass. *Statutory warning – drinking alcohol may be injurious to health.*

Khushwant Singh lived in Delhi and also had a house in the hills of Kasuali where he wrote in summers. A house in the mountains for writing. That must be the dream of every writer.

In one of his articles, Khushwant Singh mentioned that a budding writer had sent him his writings. Why not try the same, I thought.

I found Khushwant Singh's address on the internet. I was looking for his email address but could not find any. I posted him 3 short pieces and a covering letter. My articles were about questions which perhaps one grapples with when one has fewer books to study in college – life, purpose, god.

I sent the post to him, nothing happened and I forgot. Until one day when I received a postcard in my letterbox, handwritten by Khushwant Singh. I was on top of the world. He had replied, made an effort to write to me. He said my pieces made good reading and were lucid and well-worded. He also advised me not to waste arguments on such questions. This, for me, was above all of my prize winnings. I have kept the postcard, laminated and preserved.

The *Hindu* was a favourite newspaper among students preparing for competitive exams. It was dispatched from Delhi and did not reach Chandigarh before 10 am. By which time it was too late for morning readers. But I found one place where I could get scores of newspapers at the same time, even those from previous days that I had missed. It was a small public library close to where we lived.

The library was housed in a government school and opened for a couple of hours in the evenings. It had a few books and magazines and plenty of newspapers. The newspapers were placed on a reading stand, similar to a lecture stand, and had a thin metal bar in the middle to hold newspapers. I was a frequent visitor, and the sole person at times. That was one place where I experienced pin-drop (or paper-thin!) silence. One could have almost attained nirvana in the library.

In the mid-1990s, newspaper wars started in the tri-city region (Chandigarh, Panchkula and Mohali). The *Hindustan Times (HT)* and the *Times of India (ToI)* launched their Chandigarh issues. The price of newspapers went down to just Re 1. Both the newspapers started several schemes to attract customers and capture some of the market that the *Tribune* had. *HT* was giving away free bags with newspaper subscriptions,

ToI gave free Coke bottles. There were more newspapers now to choose from.

The festivals of Holi and Diwali brought along a phenomenon that can be billed as the worst nightmare of newspaper lovers. The 'no newspaper' day. Newspapers were not printed on the day of these festivals, which meant no newspapers to read the next morning. I can understand that newspaper staff need to spend time with their families. But it wasn't easy to cope with the withdrawal symptoms, I can tell you that.

Having read an unlimited number of newspapers, I tried my hand at getting my article published in a newspaper once. This was in the early noughties. I went to the hills of Shimla with a few friends from college. Gupta, Navdeep, Joshi and I. On our way to the famous Jakhoo *mandir* (Hanuman temple), our taxi driver gave up as his van was unable to climb uphill. He went away with his van, leaving the four of us in the middle of nowhere. As we started walking uphill, we looked up and saw at least 100 monkeys watching us. We froze. Even expletives, rich Punjabi expletives, could not dare to venture out.

A few monkeys approached us and started searching our pockets for food. We did not have any.

They didn't like it.

One monkey bit our dear friend Navdeep Singh. The monkey let all the rest of us go and selected him. In desperation, I took out Polo mints lying in my pocket to give it to the monkeys, which they were unable to find during our body search.

That day, in the hills of Shimla, four handsome, intelligent, young men were saved by the humble mint with the hole.

The monkeys got distracted and we walked away slowly. Pounding hearts, prayers on lips, necks dare not look back. We reached Lord Hanuman's temple safely. Well, almost.

Poor Navdeep – he had to bear the pain of a few injections afterwards. Not to mention the roasting by his friends.

Incidentally, moments before we encountered the monkeys, Navdeep had found a horseshoe made of metal lying on the road, which he had put in his pocket. Finding a horseshoe can be extremely lucky, as they say, or can bring mighty bad luck if it doesn't suit someone. Who knows. I thought it was scary, but a funny story. I typed it in double space, the requirement from newspapers, and posted it to the *Tribune*.

After a few months, the article came back by post with a note that it was not found suitable for the newspaper's requirements. I thought returning the article was a nice gesture from the newspaper. Otherwise, I would have been left in limbo wondering if or when it would be published.

While news and views are the raison d'être of a newspaper, the classifieds columns made newspapers most beneficial for practical use. Before the advent of finding things at the click of a button, people would search newspaper classifieds for houses on sale or rent, or for second-hand cars. Or go through matrimonial columns for the right match. It amazed me how explicitly the matrimonial advertisements were segregated on caste and sub-castes. And how "done computer" became the hot qualification for grooms and brides to be in those days.

If you consumed newspapers the way I did, you would have also noticed the 'change of name' notices. It was rare to find people changing their names completely. Only one word or a letter, here or there. For instance, adding an extra 'a' where just one was the norm.

"I, Balwinder Kaur, do hereby notify the change in my name to Balwinder Kaur Sekhon."

"I, Vishal Kapoor, change my name to Vishaal Kapoor."

Then there were notices of irate parents removing their ill-mannered sons from their wills, or employers announcing that they have "nothing to do" with certain former employees anymore.

Newspaper advertisements led me to enjoy other pursuits – there were many Sufi concerts tipped off by the newspapers. It irked me if reports covering the events were published the day *after* they had taken place and not advertised beforehand.

There were various concerts I attended, including Wadali brothers, Abida Parveen, Ustad Sultan Khan, a play by a Pakistani theatre group Ajoka on the life of Bulle Shah. When I attended Manna Dey performing live in Tagore Theatre in Chandigarh he was over 80. What a voice he had. Not a soul moved when he sang.

I remember how upset he became when someone in the audience requested him to sing *Dhigadha dhigi dhigi*.

"That one is from Rafi sahib," replied Manna Dey. Not even silence knew where to hide.

Newspapers also published notices of *rasam pagri* or *bhog* ceremony (obituary invitations to pay respect to the deceased). It was a bit of a shock one day to see the photo of my orthodontist, Dr Sabharwaal from Ludhiana, in the obituary section. You don't expect people you know to die.

Some newspaper columns become a part of your growing up. For instance, H. Kishie Singh's column on safe motoring in the *Tribune*. The 'Good Motoring' column has been continuing for the past 25 years or so. I learnt from his column that if on foot, you should always cross a roundabout from the narrowest part of the road. I have been following this advice since I read it, about 20 years back if not more.

Horoscopes by P. Khurrana, a famous astrologer in Chandigarh, were also a regular feature in newspapers. Nowadays of course we also know him due to his famous son, Bollywood actor Ayushmann Khurrana.

Classified advertisements by fortune tellers have become more colourful. Not long back I read a newspaper advertisement which gave an exhaustive list of problems for which one could consult the fortune teller – "child problem, visa problem, wanting job in a multinational, entrance exam problem", and hold your breath, "*sautan* problem". I will explain this to the uninitiated. Sautan = husband's paramour.

I wonder how Bauji would have reacted to newspapers full of advertisements today. Newspapers with shrinking latitude of *shudh* (pure) news. Granted he was from a different era. But the sanctity of newspapers that he believed in remains the same. The value of the written word remains the same. The joy of holding my *akhbaar* in my hand certainly remains the same.

4.

Summer Vacation

*S*ummer vacation was different from all other vacations – it was longer. Even when you combined winter vacations in December and holidays after the final exams (normally around March every year). Summer vacation lasted longer, for around 45 days in June and July. How could a child not love it?

First of all, the summer holidays were justified. Coming back home from school in afternoons, people emitting heat, literally speaking, roads so hot that you could smell charcoal and dry wind brushing past your skin giving a burning sensation. Then there were the heavy school bags to carry on our innocent shoulders. The summer vacations were absolutely justified. I am sure the teaching fraternity would concur.

However, teachers wouldn't let us have holidays without holiday homework, would they? And there was lots of it. Science, maths, social science, Hindi, Punjabi, English and even art and craft.

"You should not waste your precious holidays."

"You should work hard during your holidays."

"You should prepare for your next monthly exams during the holidays."

Yes ma'am.

The most common task was to "Write an essay on …". I think all those who went to school in India in the 1980s, throughout the length and breadth of the country, from Kashmir to Kanyakumari, from Surat to Sundarbans – if they could remember one favourite assignment by their teachers, it must be to *write an essay on …*

The essay could be on any subject – a famous personality, the best friend, the favourite TV serial, the person you liked the most, the person you hated the most (*Why would you even give such a topic to a child?*), how did you celebrate your birthday, or Independence Day or Republic Day celebrations, and so on. The list could go endless, depending on the ingenuity of the teacher. And if you were to go on a summer vacation, what best topic to ask than to write an essay on how you had spent the holidays.

After a few years of writing this essay, my sister and I had developed a standard template for the essay: I finished my reading homework in the first 15 days, the writing homework in the next 15 days and the revision in the last 15 days. This, in more detail, along with a few snippets of how we managed to get time to do one or two fun things, seemed to be a successful formula. Teachers appeared to like it. Now I must add that we did it with equal seriousness and dedication every time. Every "excellent" or "well done" signed on to our exercise books meant more marks, you see.

The truth, as you would have expected, was different. Completely different. Day 1 was no different to day 15, 30 or 45. We started doing our homework on the first day and carried on till the last. We started having fun the first day and carried on till the last.

Mom would be shouting at us to finish our homework. Now I realise why mom wanted us to be disciplined and finish our work on time. But we were helpless at that time, duty-bound by the charter of childhood.

Our Hindi and Punjabi teachers also had their favourite topic for an essay – "*Aankhon dekha mela*" or "*Akkhin ditha mela*" respectively. This was about writing a *lekh*, an essay, on a mela or a fun fair you had attended. The good thing was you that could write it in Hindi and rewrite the same essay in Punjabi or the other way around. The bad thing was that there were no melas to attend in summer. So, we borrowed melas from the other parts of the year.

Growing up in Punjab at that time you could rely on two melas – Dussehra or Vaisakhi. However, we had hardly ever attended one. Due to overcrowding at the melas and concerns around terrorism in those days, our parents avoided taking us to these celebrations. Therefore, we made up essays based on imagination, hearsay and what was shown on TV.

"All essays done, mom."

"*Chal shabaash, mera puttar*. Well done, my son. We are going to Mamaji's place tomorrow."

"Yippie!"

People normally visited their relatives and extended family during holidays. Travelling for sightseeing was not common. Not in our family anyway. Foreign travel, and that too for a vacation, was completely off the radar at that time.

We did however go to the Taj Mahal in Agra when I was seven months old and to Pahalgam (in the state of Jammu and Kashmir) when I was 3 years old, with the family of my bhuaji (dad's sister). Not that I can recall much about the visits; except a faint memory that a tube light was broken by my cousin in our hotel room in Pahalgam.

You probably did not need to know this little detail. But when you are in the warehouse of someone's memories, why not have a rummage around. Especially when you have been given permission and privileged access. You might find something interesting hidden in some corner. Plus, it allows me to preserve my memories for my future grey cells!

When I was 9 years old, we went to Shimla with the family of the eldest Mamaji (mom's brother) during the summer holidays. I enjoyed the trip to the hill station. We went horse riding, played with snow, which I had seen for the first time, and tried ice skating.

Summer vacation was probably the only time in a year when we could give focus on learning something new. Throughout an academic year in school the emphasis was primarily on studying. Extra-curricular activities were not considered important or necessary, or were entirely looked down upon. When I was around 10, our parents arranged music classes for my sister and me. A teacher would come to our house every week to teach us harmonium.

Our teacher was associated with a school for the blind in Ferozepur city. He was partially blind and would walk to our house on his own and pick up the right keys on harmonium without looking at them.

Sa re ga ma pa dha ni sa

When singing the notes, I would get conscious at the last *sa* as it is meant to be hit high. But when you are in a joint family and others are not equally inclined or appreciative musically, the high notes could irk or wake up many a *tayajis, tayijis* – the uncles and aunts – and neighbours. Not good.

Our harmonium teacher taught us many devotional and patriotic songs: *Aisi laagi lagan* by Anup Jalota, *Saare jahan se acha, Tumhi ho pata pita tumhi ho.*

He did give us the luxury of learning one Bollywood song (from the movie *Nagin*, 1954), but just the music, not the lyrics: *Mann dole mera tann dole, mere dil kya gya karaar re yeh kaun bajaaye baansuria*. I never thought I would be translating this song one day but here you go – my mind sways as does my body, who is the (snake) charmer who is playing the flute.

Dad was the first one to buy a tape recorder in our joint family. All the audio cassettes we had were of devotional songs – mostly sung by Anup Jalota, and *Hanuman Chalisa* in praise of Lord Hanuman and *Devi Vandana*, hymns of Goddess Durga. The single cassette with Bollywood songs that we had for many, many years had songs from the movie *Naseeb* (1981) on side A and *Amar Akbar Anthony* (1977) on side B.

The harmonium we had was second hand. Its key for *dha* did not work properly and gave a depressed sound. Even now if I sing the seven notes in sequence, my dha comes out depressed. That's why they say that childhood influences make us what we are. I feel sorry for my dha.

I also feel sorry that we did not carry on the music classes after that summer vacation. Perhaps mom and dad thought that we should go back to focussing on our studies. Or maybe they heeded to the joined-up advice of our joint family. We never met our music teacher again.

We did keep the harmonium for many years in the hope that I would get to play it one day. That never happened. We finally got rid of it when it was clear that *sa re ga ma* was not in a position to play a part in earning my livelihood. Having the fortune of making your passion your profession was a 'not applicable' option for most in my generation.

The motto of summer vacation however was: eat, drink, play and sleep. Memories of summer season cannot be complete without mentioning mangoes, known as the king of fruits in India. Dad brought *petis* (wooden boxes) full of mangoes in summer. He knew that it was my favourite fruit.

I also remember the biscuits that we got custom made during the vacations. We gave all the ingredients – flour, *ghee* (clarified butter made by mom) and sugar – to the bakery and got biscuits in return. The aroma of freshly baked biscuits, perched on large, metallic baking trays, the thought of warm biscuits melting on the tongue. Why wouldn't you say:

"Gar firdaus bar rue zamin ast, hamin asto, hamin asto, hamin ast"

(If there is a heaven on earth, it's here, it's here, it's here), quoting the famous 13th-century Sufi poet Amir Khusrau.

One of the charms of summer vacations was drinking sweet *lassi* (curd/yoghurt drink) during afternoons after lunch. The thing with sweet lassi is that it makes you feel drowsy, especially after a heavy lunch of *poori chhole* (fluffy, deep-fried, unleavened bread served with chickpeas curry). I felt less guilty taking afternoon naps during the vacations.

Other drinks available at that time included sugarcane juice, orange or *anaar* (pomegranate) juice, and Rooh Afza sharbat mixed with water or milk. They say that the formula of Rooh Afza has been kept secret by its manufacturers, Hamdard, for over 100 years. I will reveal it here today for you.

Pour 40 ml of Rooh Afza in a glass, add a teaspoon of sugar if you want it extra sweet (I don't recommend it), mix it, add 2 cubes of ice, pour 220 ml of water, stir the drink, bring the glass to your lips, take a small sip, hold it in your mouth for a second and then swallow. Now drink the rest of the glass in one go and say "Aaahhhh".

The fizzy drinks available in those days were Campa Cola, Thums Up, Limca and Gold Spot. The ones that could be rhymed with another word easily were favoured more (the second rhyming word is usually meaningless, though commonly used for phonetic satisfaction!).

"Would you like to have some Campa–shampa?"

"Would you like to have some Limca–shimca?"

Or the more generic version, "Would you like to have some *dhanda–shanda*?" (dhanda = cold, also meaning a cold drink)

The correct answer to the question was 'no'.

"No, no Uncleji, nothing, nothing."

And then you will be served the drink. What you were served may not necessarily be the brand you were offered in the first place. All brand names were used interchangeably to mean 'the cold drink that we have'.

There was this local soft drink in Punjab called *banta* – a fizzy soda available in a clear, glass bottle and corked using a banta (Punjabi word for a glass marble, also used for playing). I used to find it intriguing how a bottle was sealed using a banta. To pop open a bottle, the banta was pushed down and you could see gas coming out of the bottle. The drink was served with a squeeze of lemon, black pepper, salt and ice.

If you were travelling on a hot summer afternoon, on a Punjab Roadways bus, a glass of chilled banta at a bus stop would most definitely recharge your bones – all 206 of them. However, it was considered unhygienic. So, *ache bache*, nice children, rarely got to drink it. Until they grew up and started to travel on their own. Ha.

There were several indoor games we got to learn during summer vacations. Ludo, snakes and ladders, Chinese checkers, carrom board, chess and cards. When the heat subsided during evenings, we would go out to play cricket or at times *pithu garam*.

Have you played pithu garam? Children would gather in the streets, form two teams and pile a few flat stones on top of each other on the ground. A player from one team would hit the stones with a ball and other players of the team had to put the stones back together without getting caught (that's just the gist of it). It was fun.

That was the time when video games were launched and had become quite a craze. You could hear Mario being played in every corner of the bazaars. Video game parlours, that's what the shops were called, became a favourite hunting ground for children in no time. Needless to say, ache bache were not allowed to play video games. I felt upset at that time for not getting to play video games. But I am now glad that at least in my childhood I was not dependent on screens.

Summer vacations were also the time for me to read new books. Books that were not related to school work. And what best than to have a library at home?

Bauji (my grandfather) had his own library at our ancestral house where I used to read books. Getting it issued from Bauji was somewhat tricky. He would note down the name of the book, its serial number (which he had given), author's name, issue date and my name.

Bauji had migrated to the Indian Punjab from Pakistan during Partition in 1947. Bauji and Biji (my grandmother) had two tayajis (my dad's elder brothers) with them when they moved to India. My dad was born in India in 1948, and his sister a couple of years later.

Those who migrated during Partition settled wherever they could. At times it was determined by the location of a relative or a friend in India, or if they knew someone who knew someone somewhere in India, or the nearest place next to the border between India and Pakistan (if people knew where exactly the border was). Some just relied on wherever the government camps could rehabilitate them or wherever their animal carts, trains or feet took them. Millions were estimated to be displaced, went missing, kidnapped, raped or died during Partition.

Bauji first went to Jalandhar city where his sister lived along with her husband. That's where my dad was born. They later moved to Ferozepur city, where Bauji stayed all his life. I wish I had got to spend more time with him and listen to his stories of Partition and what it was like before that. He passed away a few years ago, at nearly 90 years of age.

Bauji was well respected, fondly known by those around him as Bhagatji. (The literal translation of *bhagat* is 'devotee'. Bhagatji is normally used as a mark of respect to address someone who is respected as a religious or spiritual figure – a guru, a preacher or a priest.)

Although he worked as a *tehsildar* (revenue officer) in Ferozepur, he delivered sermons in temples, gurudwaras, schools and government offices on spirituality and moral and national responsibility.

He was well-read, often quoting Bhagwad Gita, Ramayan, Guru Granth Sahib, the Quran and the Bible, apart from many other spiritual texts and gurus.

We, and everyone who knew him, would greet him, "Raam raam, Bauji" and he would reply "Raam raam ... raam raam".

He slept at 7 pm, woke up at 3:30 am, took a bath with water kept overnight in a tub, went to the temple nearby at 4:40 am, delivered a sermon to his followers and came back home at 6:15 am, along with some of the devotees. That's when we would wake up and run helter-skelter so that he didn't find us asleep.

Bauji followed this routine every day, summer or winter, for the last 50 years of his life. He illuminated the lives of those around him.

He used to call me 'handpump'. *"Eh jinna zameen de uppar hai, uss ton zaada zameen de andar hai"* (He is much deeper under the ground than above it), he used to say.

I enjoyed numerous afternoons spent in Bauji's library, absorbed in books, which were mainly spiritual, and mythological stories of kings and queens, all emphasising moral values and good deeds. The books were in Hindi, Punjabi, English, or Urdu. Bauji was fluent in all these languages. I could read the other languages but not Urdu, although I could understand the language as we spoke a mixture of Hindi, Punjabi and Urdu words in everyday life.

The afternoons spent in Bauji's library during summer vacations remain for me the epitome of my childhood.

To Bauji.

And to all other stars like him, shining bright, who endured loss beyond belief, stood up, and reigned over the kingdom of life.

5.

Visiting Mamaji's

*V*isiting extended family during vacations was the in thing. With mom having three brothers (my *mamajis*) and two sisters (my *maasijis*), our options were aplenty. Visits to the mamajis' families were more frequent. All our mamajis had children the similar age as my sister and me. Which meant we never got bored during our visits.

The eldest Mamaji would organise several family get-togethers. They were friends with our school principal and invited him along with his family to the parties. I would feel awkward, though delighted, to see our school principal at our family gatherings. My dad first started drinking alcohol at one such gathering, I have been told.

Mamaji had a VCR when we were little. We would watch endless movies at his place, a number of them over and over again. We would have seen *Namak Halaal* (1982) about 50 times if not more. They also had a large collection of video cassettes of Tom and Jerry, which Mamaji seemed to like as well.

I used to be surprised to see Mamaji watching Tom and Jerry with interest. He was a mamaji after all. But I think now I know what made him like cartoons. These days I can watch animated movies (not 3D) for hours. There's something ageless, innocent, and detached from the real world about cartoons.

My sister and I would also spend time reading and finishing holiday homework, along with our cousins. We spent most of the time indoors as Mamaji's house was next to a busy road. I listened to my first English song at their place, a well-known number by Cliff Richards released in 1963:

We're all goin' on a summer holiday
No more workin' for a week or two
Fun and laughter on a summer holiday
No more worries for me or you
For a week or two.

Once an act of nature forced us to visit Mamaji's house. Large areas of Punjab were flooded in 1988, in what was perhaps the worst floods in the region. This happened due to heavy rains and some fault at the Bhakra Dam at river Sutlej.

The flooding was an incredible experience. People knew that water was about to reach our city, Ferozepur. There was a countdown in our street – 5 hours left, 2 hours left, 1 hour left. Everyone bought their rations to keep going for a few days. That probably was the first time I had tasted condensed milk (Nestlé Milkmaid it was I think).

People in our street had built a wall using sandbags to prevent water from flowing into the street. The night when water was expected in our area, power was cut off. People used candles, torches, lanterns to do final preparations and bolster the sand wall. It must have been past midnight that the wait was finally over. I witnessed flood water flowing out through the *naalis* (open, narrow drains) into our street.

There were shouts of "water's here!" and everyone rushed back to their houses. When we woke up the next morning, our street was submerged under nearly 3 feet of water. *So, this is what they call a flood*, I thought.

Little did I know that the aftermath of a flood was the most challenging bit. Water started subsiding after a couple of days. People started venturing out, either using small boats or just rolling up their trousers and walking carefully. An outbreak of cholera followed and we were given injections to safeguard against that.

This was the time when my parents decided that we should go to Mamaji's house, who lived in a nearby city which was not affected by flooding. So, mom, my sister and I went and stayed there for a week or so, till things became better back home. Dad could not join us due to his work.

Mamaji had a car, the first one in our extended family. It was a green Fiat. In those days there was hardly any variety in cars in India. If you said Fiat, everyone knew what you meant as there was just one model. Same with Ambassador, Contessa or Maruti.

All of us, all 8 of us – from Mamaji's family and our family – would fit in their 5-seater car and drive to *Nanaji* and *Naniji's* place (mom's father and mother, whom we addressed as *Pitaji* and *Mataji* respectively). The second Mamaji and his family also lived with them.

The journey to their place was no more than an hour, but it was fun. We passed through various villages and farms, greeted by hanging, retort-shaped nests made by weaver birds lined up on the way.

There weren't any seat belts in those days – or at least I do not recall anyone wearing them. The second Mamaji knew that I liked *jalebis*. Therefore, those super-sweet jalebis were always made available when we arrived.

Some of you might know about an old tradition in Punjab

whereby some Hindu families raised their eldest son as a follower of Sikhism. This tradition was observed in mom's family. Pitaji followed Hinduism and his brother adopted Sikhism. My extended family from mom's side still follows both religions as a way of life.

Pitaji had a shop selling cloth and textiles. The second Mamaji inherited the shop. I would accompany Mamaji to the shop and spent many long summer afternoons watching how to unpack and pack rolls of cloth. I found it fascinating and learnt how to handle the rolls.

Mamaji and his staff were adept at dealing with customers. Many of them were ladies looking for cloth for making *salwar kameez* (a common, traditional outfit for women in South Asia). Some of the customers would leave us frustrated by asking us to unpack many rolls, showing disinterest in each one of them and not buying anything in the end. Those who did buy would haggle. Few paid the price they were quoted. Few were in any hurry to leave. I guess Mamaji would have factored that in his pricing in the first place.

Mamaji had a neighbour who owned a 'tempu', a vintage Bajaj Tempo. It was a three-wheeler, an elongated version of the modern-day three-wheeler (auto-rickshaw). It was commonly used in rural Punjab to transport people.

When this neighbour came back home in the evening, all children in the street would jump onto his tempu and he would give us a short ride. There was a shelf at the back of the tempu where the children would stand. I wonder if I will be able to do that adventure now. Probably not. A child has the advantage of innocence on their side, without inhibitions of adulthood.

At times we took a train to reach the town where Pitaji lived. Dad would drop us to the train station on scooter. Or we took a rickshaw. Sometimes dad accompanied us for a few days, but mostly it was mom, my sister and I who went, particularly when we were visiting for a week or two during vacations.

The train took not more than 45 minutes. There were 4 stations en route – about 10 to 15 minutes away from each other. The train's siren, the sound of chugging, the smell of coal, the wind that touched your face, the rectangular cardboard tickets, everything that now seems so surreal, was exciting. Perhaps these train journeys cultivated my love towards trains and vintage steam trains in particular.

Someone from Mamaji's family was usually present at the train station at the other end to pick us up. Or we hired a rickshaw.

One thing with rickshaw pullers was that no one ever gave them the fare they had asked for. If they asked for Rs 5 (which was a good sum of money then), people would start from Rs 3, haggle for some time and then settle at Rs 4. I cannot remember a single rickshaw journey where no haggling was involved. When I did first rickshaw journey on my own, I tried haggling, but without success. So, I stopped bothering at all.

Sometimes, the third (the youngest) Mamaji and his family also joined us at Pitaji's house. So, now in this one house there were 4 families and 9 children. Similar ages. What do you expect? Cacophony.

We had plenty of things to do, sometimes too many. We would end up playing good old hide-and-seek, pillow fighting (which at times turned real), playing carrom board, helping Mamiji and mom in cooking or cleaning the house, visiting nearby rice shellers, ice cream factories, or other relatives in the town.

Tuesday evenings were reserved for visiting the local temple to listen to Hanuman Chalisa and for Tuesday-special *boondi ka prasad* (small sweet balls made of gram flour used as offerings/

oblations). The mandir we attended was famous for 'Jajjal Waali Mata', a woman who achieved the status of a deity in that region and is still revered.

The youngest Mamaji lived in Jalandhar (Punjab). It was a huge city for me at that time, compared to ours. I remember being awed at the Jalandhar Doordarshan building when I saw it for the first time. *So, this was where everything on our TV was broadcast from*, I thought.

I would accompany Mamaji to his factory where he manufactured metal taps. We would call Mamaji "*patake waale Mamaji*" because he would pull our fingers which produced a cracking sound from the knuckles (*patake* being crackers).

I also remember Mamaji bringing 'Fatafat' for us whenever we met. We loved it. Fatafat, if you are not aware, is a brand of ayurvedic digestive pills. But we just enjoyed it as spicy, tangy candy balls. Do try it.

Leaving any mamaji's house was a ritual of its own. Mamaji would pick up our luggage. Some form of transport was made available outside the house, if we did not have our own. Mostly a rickshaw or three-wheeler. We would be about to leave the front door when Mamiji would bring some gifts, mostly clothes and some cash.

Now there was a proper way of doing this. Non-cash gifts were usually accepted, with some *nahi-nahi* (no-no) at times but not too much. Not for cash. A lot of fuss was made about it. The cash would pass from Mamiji's hands to mom's hands to Mamiji's children, back to Mamiji and then it would end up either with my sister or me. And Mamaji coaxing Mamiji all this time.

When you are a child watching all this 'cash transfer', you think this must be some bad cash. So, you should not keep it. Therefore, we gave it to our mom. Then the second round began;

this time to reduce the amount of cash. Somehow things got settled. The whole 'this' took no more than a minute or so.

After saying goodbyes, when we were in rickshaw heading towards the train station, mom would say that this was the circle of life – you take some, you give some. Which we did whenever dad's sister or other relatives came to ours.

Later, our family moved to Chandigarh and visits to Mamaji's started becoming fewer because of the longer distances involved. I guess also because there were no summer vacations anymore as all my cousins left school, got busy settling down in their careers, started getting married and having children one by one. But memories of visiting Mamaji's, of the carefree days, remain tucked away somewhere innocent.

6.

Power Cuts

*H*omi J. Bhabha (1909–1966), known as father of the Indian nuclear programme, said, "No power is as costly as no power." He must be among a handful of people who called it 'power'. We called it 'light' or *bijli* (electricity).

Light *jaana* (power cut) and light *aana* (power restored) were events in life. And they happened daily. Power cuts reinforced our acceptance of all things as they are. They were a daily reminder that things were not in your hands. The bijli *mehkma* (electricity board) was almighty.

Power cuts would vary, from a few minutes to a few hours and in extreme cases for a whole day. Power cuts had the habit of happening when you needed electricity the most – in summers. Scorching air, people getting roasted, life coming to a standstill in afternoons. All you wanted was to go home, have chilled Rooh Afza prepared by mom, and sleep under the fan or run the desert cooler. Air conditioners happened late.

Coming home from school to a power cut was the biggest disappointment. Apart from having to suffer in the heat, you also had to miss Doordarshan's afternoon TV transmission.

At times mom would comfort us using a *pakkhi* (hand fan) while my sister and I had our lunch during a power cut. These fans were made of cloth or bamboo.

What would you do after having lunch during a power cut? Take a nap, and hope that light was back soon. Sometimes it did while we were asleep. This was the most pleasant experience. A gentle breeze started flowing in the room as fans or desert coolers got switched on while we slept. Mosquitoes would also stop troubling. Heaven.

Desert coolers had a special significance in our family's yearly calendar. Just before the arrival of summer we would get our cooler out from its winter hibernation and give it a complete wash.

We also got new cooling pads (made of wood shavings) for the cooler. Dad and I would jump on our Bajaj Chetak and get cooling pads for the three doors that the cooler had. That was a huge, grey, metal cooler we had. We would clean it, fill it with water and stick it next to our room window. The first cool air of the season ready for you.

After a few years of enjoying the cooler, I realised that coolers do not have to be grey, huge and metallic. They also started coming in cream, in small sizes and in plastic. One became two and then three coolers, one for each room. All different shapes and sizes, all different colours. I think one of them was bought by us and two were given to us by State Bank of India where dad worked.

The bank gave furniture and some household items to staff as most employees were transferred to a different location every 3 years or so. My friend Joshi would get piqued by the fact that dad's employer provided us with various household stuff. *Sorry Joshi, we had no choice but to avail the facility.*

While I liked desert coolers, I liked fans more. Ceiling fans had five different settings (1 to 5) while coolers normally had three (high, mid, low). Coolers would make it too cold at times. Ceiling fans had that traditional, homely feel and would make you fall asleep more quickly. They were less noisy and farther away from you. Not to mention the fact that you could tie balloons and decorations on ceiling fans at birthday parties.

Have you heard of this Hindi children's rhyme, inspired by ceiling fans?

Oopar pankha chalta hai,
Neeche baby sota hai.
Sote sote bhookh lagi,
Khaalo beta moongfli.
Moongfli mein dana nahi,
Hum tumahre mama nahi.
Mama gaye dilli,
Wahan se laye billi.
Billi ne maara panja,
Mama ho gya ganja.
Bille ke doh bache,
Hum sab sache.

If I were to search for one composition whose literal translation wouldn't make much sense, it is this. It's a collection of rhyming couplets, not necessarily following a single theme. I would therefore limit myself here by saying that the rhyme starts with talking about a baby who is sleeping underneath a ceiling fan...

Now that we have paused for a lyrical break, let me narrate another story. A few years back I asked my friend Datta: "Datte, do you think God exists?"

He replied, "Yes. Otherwise, we wouldn't have this song – *rabba rabba meeh varsa, saadi kothi daane paa*" (O God, make it rain; let our bungalow be abound with grains). Nice logic, wouldn't you agree?

Let's carry on. In those days, pedestal fans (also called *farrata* fans) were in demand. They were normally used at weddings or religious or political gatherings. They were huge, clunky fans imprisoned in round, metal frames. They stood there as if they owned the time and space.

Now, what would you do when it is late in the evening, and you have to finish your homework and a power cut happens? Or worse still, if it is your exam the next day? During childhood, we would deploy a kerosene lamp for rescue. Remove the lantern's glass chimney, roll up the wick using a knob located at the base of the lamp, light it and put the chimney back. It may sound medieval but that was how it was in the early 1980s.

Then there was always a humble candle ready to light up your academic path. I had learnt in science class in school that you can put a candle in front of a mirror to get more light per candle. This tip helped us during many a power cut.

Mom used to tell us a story that the late Prime Minister Lal Bahadur Shastri studied in the light of *jugnus* (firefly) and walked a few kilometres without shoes every day to go to school as his family did not have enough resources. *How did he carry his heavy school bag for that distance*, I would wonder.

Later, we acquired a handheld battery-powered tube light. The battery was charged whenever power was available. The tube light was the size of the usual one-litre water bottle, having two small tube lights and a flashing, orange-coloured siren. We would switch on the siren for fun but made sure we did not overuse it as we needed to make sure that the battery remained charged for use during a power cut.

Studying under the tube light was not easy. It meant that both my sister and I had to sit along with our books around the small device. Not to mention the houseflies wanting a share of our light, or mosquitoes using the opportunity to teach feeding skills to their offspring.

When power cuts felt lazy, they would send their half-cousin, low voltage instead. The thing with low voltage was that it was annoying. The poet Ghalib said, "*Mujhe kya bura tha marna, agar ek baar hota ...*" (I would have happily died if it was just once). Similarly, you did not want low voltage hovering over you time and again; you were better off with no power at all. There was at least a hope that someone, somewhere would try to fix it, sooner.

Low voltage arrived in a set sequence. First, a power cut happened, then the light came back after a while but with a low voltage. Then a power cut happened again. Finally, you got light back with full voltage. The gap between each step could be a few minutes or a few hours.

Our ancestral house in Ferozepur had one bulb in the verandah. One yellow-light emitting bulb in a big verandah, surviving on low voltage on a late summer evening could have single-handedly triggered depression. Fortunately, there were many people around in our joint family for any adverse psychological impact of a single faint bulb.

At times we had a fluctuation in voltage. Low voltage one minute and a sudden surge next minute. When this happened, we had to make sure to switch off all electrical appliances else they could be damaged. We would leave one bulb switched on to know when the normal voltage returned. Ah, I knew the bulb in our verandah had some use!

The electrical devices in those days were mainly tube lights or bulbs, fans, radios and later, TVs. No mobile phones, laptops, ACs, microwaves or cooking hobs. Refrigerators were also late entrants. Given the choice to protect any of these devices from voltage fluctuation, I would go for radio – especially the Murphy radio we had in those days. *Remember its logo, the Murphy baby?*

As I grew up, we moved out of the joint family house to our own place. In this house, we had a stabiliser installed to steady the voltage in case of fluctuation. Boosters were used for load-heavy devices such as TV and refrigerator. So, now when the voltage was low the stabiliser kicked in and brought back the voltage to its normal level.

People started purchasing generators to deal with power cuts. My eldest mamaji bought a generator for his house. I was as much fascinated as I was scared of the machine. It was the size of a lion, standing upright at the rooftop of Mamaji's house. It was a momentous occasion for me whenever a power cut occurred during our visit to Mamaji's place. I knew Mamaji would switch it on and I could witness that ceremony.

The generator was run on diesel and had a manual lever which you had to jack into the main machine and rotate a number of times till it started puffing smoke out. Then you had to pull the lever out, and fast. Once running, it gave a rhythmic, majestic sound. How exciting for a young one to watch.

However, its manual operation scared me. What if you were not able to rotate the lever with enough force? What if you were not able to pull out the lever in time once the generator had started? Would it throw you off at a distance?

Fortunately, I didn't have to operate it. Benefits of being a child. Mamaji, on the other hand, did not have that luxury. Once he was attempting to start the generator but was not able to remove the lever quickly enough. He ended up with a fractured arm unfortunately.

You would understand, therefore, why I was so relieved to see the new era of generators – small, light, easy to operate Shriram Hondas. Just pull a thin wire and there you go. They were not as powerful as the manual ones but at least they were safer. We, however, never had a generator at our house.

We got an 'invertor' instead. This was a battery that charged when power was available and provided electricity during a power cut. Silent, no pollution and automatic. Marvellous. But the battery was not powerful enough, we just had a few devices powered by it. A couple of tube lights or bulbs, and a fan. You couldn't run luxury items – TV, fridge, and the like on an inverter.

Some electricity meters also supported multiple 'phases'. Electricity connections in different parts of the house were divided into different sections or phases. We had 3 phases. A power cut at times affected one or two phases and spared the rest. I am not sure who should get credit for this technology – some inventor in some university, the bijli board or my dad. It was a relief. At least one room could have light during a power cut.

People accepted their fate if the entire neighbourhood had the power cut. But if you were the only house or among one or two houses that had suffered a power cut, life suddenly felt unfair.

It was completely normal to go to your neighbour's house for a few hours if they had light and you did not, and you had exams to prepare for. It was acceptable to do the same during unmissable events such as the telecast of Mahabharat or Ramayan on TV. Live cricket matches were also treated as a valid reason.

During a power cut, you could see an army of children deployed by parents to find out if any home in the neighbourhood was still graced with power. And what power it was. The whole street descended to that lucky house, uninvited yes but no one seemed to mind. It all seemed natural, normal.

Power cuts during winters were fewer. However, they did happen in the early mornings at times which meant that we could not use our electric geyser for hot water when getting ready for school. Mom and dad would heat water for us on the gas stove, one *pateela* (large pan) at a time, so that we could take our baths. *Thank you, both, for giving us a comfortable childhood.*

With all these experiences with power cuts, no wonder I retain the habit of switching off lights and other electric devices as soon as they are not needed. Save it, to have it, and to share it. *Overconsumption, just because it can be afforded, is not going to leave the planet a happy place.*

What do you do when there is no light, and no exams? Go out and mingle with neighbours. Power cuts created a bonhomie on streets, particularly in summer evenings when the hot sun had given way to a cool breeze. People would come out of their houses, chat with each other, and share a meal when power cuts happened. All age groups were welcome. Grandparents having their discussions, parents sharing laughs and children getting an excuse to play outside.

When we moved to Chandigarh, I found out that timings of power cuts in the city were announced daily in local newspapers. The certainty was definitely helpful to plan your day. But not as much fun. Or shall we say *no power was as much fun as no power.*

7.

PP Number

While the world may know PP as pay phone, for us it was *padosi's* phone (neighbour's phone).

During my childhood, telephone connections were rare. There was a long waiting list – sometimes years to get a connection. Phones meant landline phones; no mobiles, no broadband, no SMS. All this might seem alien to the millennials today but this was life until recently.

DoT – the Department of Telecom – was the sole provider. DoTliness was next to godliness. And linemen were anointed angels. Who can revive a dead man and a dead phone but angels.

My earliest memory of a phone goes back to the early 1980s. One family in our street had a phone connection. Their number was our PP number, and everyone else's in the street. They had two entrances to their house, one for the main house and one for the room with the phone – convenient for them and convenient for the whole street.

The phone was stationed on a small table that was sandwiched between two single sofa seats. It was an old rotary dial phone, black in colour, as most phones were in those days. The circular dial with the digits 0 to 9 marked along its circumference. The dial had a round, hollow space corresponding to each digit where you could fit your finger to move the dial.

You dialled the required digit by rotating the dial clockwise to the extreme right. The dial made two different sounds – one when you dialled a digit, and the second when you left the dial to come back to its original position after dialling. '0' would take the longest to dial and to come back, '1' would take the smallest amount of time.

The phone had a small white sticker to write down the telephone number, which was protected by a transparent plastic cover. The phone numbers were short at that time – 4 digits. Somehow the number 2802 rings a bell! I think that was our PP number. It was not a pay phone. We were not paying money to our neighbours. But they did earn something out of it.

The family with a phone had a special, elevated status in their *mohalla* (neighbourhood). People would be careful not to pick up an argument with them. So what if their child beat yours – they have the telephone. So what if they park their scooter in front of your house – they have the telephone. So what if their *dadi* (grandmother) throws a bucket load of water on children playing cricket in the street because her afternoon nap is being disturbed – they, ladies and gentlemen, have the telephone.

PP number was a fully acceptable mode of communication and was given as the contact number in application forms for public utilities or schools or jobs.

Name: Om Prakash
Address: Chaudhari Lal Di Haveli, Pakka Mohalla, Ferozepur city, Punjab
Pin code: 152002
Telephone: 2802 (PP)

PP number was used mainly for receiving calls, and hardly ever for making a call. Every time the phone rang, the owners must have hoped that this time the call was meant for them. But on the other end, some caller asked for "Guddi da munda", "Subhash da bhateeja" (Guddi's son, Subhash's nephew).

People would ring a PP number, ask for a particular person from the neighbourhood, disconnect the call and ring back again, giving enough time for the person to arrive. It must have been tough in hot, sunny afternoons to fetch a neighbour when most people at home would be taking a nap.

Phone owners often sat there listening to neighbours' conversations. Privacy was not a part of the social contract. It was their phone after all.

One of my mamajis (mom's brother) introduced the young me to a fascinating device – an intercom. Mamaji's house was spread over two floors. They had their residence on the first floor, and their clinic on the ground floor where Mamiji (Mamaji's wife) used to practise as a doctor. They had one telephone connection, and phone points in various rooms, upstairs and downstairs to communicate with each other during the day. I used to be captivated by the fact that you can communicate between different parts of the house using a device like an intercom.

In the morning, Mamiji used to take their telephone to her clinic on the ground floor. And it came up with her to their residence on the first floor in the evening.

An interesting incidence is connected to their phone connection. This was the time when they moved their residence to a new house given by the hospital where Mamaji worked. It was in the same city, and Mamiji's clinic remained at the old location. The phone now permanently stayed at the clinic.

Mamiji's brother, who also lived in the same town, started receiving threats to kill Mamiji. This continued for a few days.

The situation in Punjab at that time was unsettled, to say the least. Life threats and kidnappings happened. So everyone in the family was scared because of the phone calls.

Mamiji's brother thought that the person making the threatening calls sounded like a woman. When he asked the caller who she was, the caller said that she was not a 'she' but a 'he'. This put some doubt in his mind.

Another pattern was noted – the phone calls were received solely during the afternoon, between 1 pm and 3 pm. And were made to Mamiji's brother and not to Mamiji herself. The adults in the family who were dealing with this were all intelligent folk – doctors, lawyers, educationists, bankers. They decided to investigate on their own.

According to the plan, my mom was locked in one of the rooms in the clinic early in the morning, before anyone arrived. She had to stay quiet and hidden. Then Mamiji arrived, her staff arrived, and so did the patients. The day progressed as usual. Mamiji left at lunchtime as she normally did. Her brother received the phone call again – "sodh dyaange" (we'll kill her).

Only this time my mom, my clever mom, was listening. Yes, the call was being made from the clinic itself.

Mamiji came back from lunch, mom came out from the hiding place and the plot was unearthed. It so happened that one of the staff members at the clinic was upset at Mamiji for apparently scolding her over something a few days back. This was her idea of taking revenge, by merely scaring Mamiji.

The staff member did not have access to any other telephone – just the one in the clinic. So she used this phone when Mamiji went for lunch. She knew Mamiji's brother's telephone number. Hence the calls were made to him. She used a cloth to muffle her voice and pretended that she was a man.

Disguising of voice by covering the handset using a

handkerchief has been used in many Bollywood plots. At least it was not as bad as another famous method of disguise used in Bollywood movies – putting an artificial mole on your cheek and pretending that no one recognises you. Interestingly nobody did – until the mole was removed for the benefit of the unsuspecting heroine.

Bollywood's love affair with the telephone was portrayed in many movies, be it the famous song from the movie *Patanga* (1949), "*Mere piya gaye Rangoon, wahan se kiya hai telephone*" (My love went to Rangoon and called me from over there). Or cross-connection on Babu Rao's phone (enacted so brilliantly by Paresh Rawal) creating a comedy of errors in *Hera Pheri* (2000).

I have spent my childhood watching people shout on the telephone. Maybe the sound was not very clear in those days, or perhaps people thought that that's the way to talk on phone. Everyone shouted at the top of their voice. Some elderly people still do it. It became a habit for them I suppose.

Another peculiar feature was nodding your head while greeting somebody on phone, even though you knew you couldn't be seen by the person on the other end.

Getting a phone connection was a big event in life, which was duly celebrated. There was anticipation and excitement in the air. When the phone finally arrived, the lineman, who had come to install the phone was treated like a celebrity. They were offered *chai paani* (a token of thanks) which may have at times taken the shape of a currency note or two, oblivious to everyone involved, naturally.

Life around telephone connections is captured with brilliance in Jaspal Bhatti's *Flop Show*, which was perhaps one of the best satire programmes on Indian national television. In one of the episodes, when a phone connection is installed in Jaspal Bhatti's house, 7 years after applying for it, they celebrate it in the manner as was typically done in Indian households when I was growing up – women sitting together, singing and playing *dholki* (a two-sided musical drum), tapping the dholki with a spoon to keep track of the beat, *mithai* (sweets) being served and men standing around the house chatting and having drinks.

Bhatti's phone number becomes the PP number for his neighbours. One neighbour gets the phone number printed on his visiting cards. The neighbour's daughter gives the phone number to her boyfriend. She wants to marry that guy but her father wants her to marry "lineman sir" of their area (played beautifully by Vivek Shauq) because of the importance of linemen in life.

One particular scene in this episode deserves special mention. It was hilarious. The lineman asks his assistant to go to the girl's house on his behalf and take some fruit with him as a gift. The assistant does that. He goes to her house, finds the girl's parents and Bhatti and his wife sitting there on the sofa, and says that the lineman has sent some fruit. He gives them a bunch of *ganne* (sugarcane stalk). And everyone acts normal. It is a must-watch.

I know I digress at times. But that's because I don't want you to miss out on anything.

Moving on, the 1990s brought a revolution – STD PCOs. This famous personality commands its full name as Subscriber Trunk Dialling Public Call Office. Essentially, a commercial payphone. You pay to call.

In those days, few people had the facility to make a distance call (that is, STD or what was also called a trunk call in yesteryears), from their home telephone. Hardly anyone had ISD or international subscriber dial – the facility to call internationally. The calls were rather expensive. So the PCOs started to be used. They sprung up everywhere. Every market had one, then two, three and many more.

In our neighbourhood, two houses had a PCO. The houses were directly opposite each other. One of the PCO owners alleged that the other one does some hanky panky with his *bhabhi* (sister-in-law). I cannot vouch for that. They had converted their front rooms as PCOs and fought all the time with each other to attract customers.

Every evening the PCOs got crowded. Some people sitting, some standing around the phone, all in the same room, listening to each other's conversations. We ended up using the PCOs frequently during those days. Our family was spread over different regions at that time – my dad was stationed in the state of Himachal Pradesh for his work, my sister was studying in Punjab and mom and I were in Chandigarh where I was studying. Our telephone connection at home did not have the facility to make inter-state calls. So PCOs became an essential mode of communication for us.

The lines would get pretty busy in the evenings.

"Iss route ki sabhi lineayn vyast hain, kripya thodi der baad daayal karein, dhanyawaad." All lines in this route are busy, please dial after some time, thank you.

The traffic eased out after 9:30 pm.

The words STD PCO were always written in red. I once saw a note outside a PCO saying *"Lo kallo baat"*, the famous dialogue by Amitabh Bachchan from the comedy movie *Namak Halaal* (1982). How creative, I thought. (The literal meaning of the correct pronunciation – *lo kar lo baat* – is 'go on, have a chat'. But it is also used as a statement of surprise or dissatisfaction or sarcasm as was done in the movie with a comical effect.)

Dr Manmohan Singh, as the finance minister under the Narasimha Rao government, ushered in economic reforms in 1991. Dr Singh quoted Victor Hugo in his now-famous budget speech that year – "No power on earth can stop an idea whose time has come." And voila, things did start changing in India after that.

When we got our first telephone connection in Chandigarh in 1994, the waiting list was just 3 months long. I was so pleasantly surprised. Our phone, not PP, not Mamaji's, in just 3 months, not years.

However, it took a couple of days after installation for the phone to become operational. The wait was killing. I would keep checking over and over again for the dial tone. Our beautiful, new, cream phone with black push buttons was lying there in zen meditation. To hear the sound of the dial tone was all I wanted.

After our phone started working, it took some time before our contacts got to know about our phone and started calling us. So the phone hardly rang at the start. This is not what you want. You want to hear the phone ring, again and again.

The phones had the facility of calling a special number, which rang you back. It was an automated call that was used to check if the phone line was working. There was no one on the other end to talk back – obviously. I rang this number over and over again, just to hear our phone ring.

When you are in college, you meet compatible folk with whom you need to exchange 'notes' frequently. This can be tricky to do when you are at your home, especially for those like me who find it uncomfortable talking on phone in front of anyone else. When our phone rang and I had spent some time on the call, with my room door closed, dad would ask: "Whose call was it?"

"Mine", I would reply.

8.

Cricket

I was very young when Kapil Dev and his team won the 1983 Cricket World Cup. What a win it must have been. Winning the world cup in England, beating the mighty West Indies in the final. India made 183 runs in the first innings and still beat West Indies, restricting them to 140.

As the anecdote goes, Kapil Dev told his teammates in the dressing room during lunch break, *"Humne 183 bana liye hain, unhon ne banane hain"* (We have scored 183 runs, they still have to). How powerful. How charged the dressing room must have been that day.

Earlier in the world cup, Kapil Dev scored a massive 175 runs in the group match against Zimbabwe which kept India in the running. Sadly, the BBC was on strike that day and no video footage of the innings is available.

The world cup win would have bolstered the spirits of the nation like no other. Cricket already held a special place in India's heart. The game was played on every street, every *mohalla* (neighbourhood) and every ground available. Matches were played during the evenings, weekends, summer holidays and at any time when a willing bunch of people (or just two players) were available.

You can say that all this is still true. But we had more time to play in those days. We didn't have mobile phones to occupy our free time and there was a single TV channel with a limited number of programmes.

All *galis* (streets) and mohallas had different rules. A try ball was the first ball to a batsman to allow them to test the waters, and they couldn't be given out on that ball.

A *vatta* ball, a dead ball, was usually reserved if some player's younger brother or sister started to cry and had to be given the bat at the behest of their mom. Some such siblings would get greedy and didn't want to leave it at one ball, frustrating all other players.

One-bounce-catch-out was another rule, normally used if the number of players was large, or the time to play the match was limited, or the ground (or street) was small. At times the rules were put in place just because a more powerful or dominating child wanted it that way.

Sometimes there were no runs behind the wicket, or runs solely on the left (or right) hand side were counted. These rules were applied normally when the number of players was small. The batsman was made responsible for getting the ball back if it went behind the wicket. Or you could have just *chaukka chhakka*, a four or a six, if you hit behind the wicket or one side of the wicket. At times you could simply 'run' for the runs and not hit any chaukka or chhakka.

The runner would become the umpire, notwithstanding the conflict of interest. Fielding was shared, which meant both teams fielded in both innings. Arguments and fighting happened when someone fielded badly when their team was batting.

But first things first. Captains were decided at the beginning, who then selected their teams. Who will be the captain? Either the eldest kid, or the one with the best built, or the loudest or the one who brought the bat, or a mixture of some of these criteria. Occasionally, consideration was also given to batting and/or balling skills.

Sumit *Bhaiya*, the elder brother to one and all, would declare himself the captain. He and the other captain then picked up their trusted soldiers, one by one. Like a captain, a player could also be selected on various criteria – a) a good batsman and/ or bowler b) a close friend of Sumit Bhaiya, c) of the same age group as Sumit Bhaiya (or at least not elder than Sumit Bhaiya), d) Sumit Bhaiya's *bhuaji's* (aunt's) son who was a visitor from Jalandhar (most likely in summer holidays), e) the one who gave a good birthday present to Sumit Bhaiya, f) the one who didn't disclose to Sumit Bhaiya's mom that he started a fight in the school or g) the younger brother of Sumit Bhaiya and if they hadn't had an argument in the last couple of days.

The concept of '*relu katta*' played a special role in team formation. It's a Punjabi word, which in local cricket was used for someone who played for both teams. I am not aware of its equivalent term in Hindi. Neither am I aware of its equivalent term in English.

The idea of relu katta in cricket should be fully researched. It encompasses many principles – management of human resources, human rights, loyalty, impartiality, psychological impact and motivation.

The need for a relu katta arose when an extra player had to be accommodated after the two teams had selected an equal number of players. "*Tu relu katta ban ja*" – you can become a relu katta – must be the most demeaning words in cricket history.

How a relu katta was selected depended on the method of selecting the teams in the first place. It was less common to have relu kattas in 'professional' gali matches as the teams would have been decided in advance. In any case, if an extra player was available, it would be up to Sumit Bhaiya, the captain, to decide who the relu katta shall be.

You could also become a relu katta if you were late and the match had already started. Or if your mom had asked Sumit Bhaiya to include you in the team; which he didn't want to but had to if he did not want a face-off with Auntyji.

If players were from different streets, team formation was easy. Everyone from Kumaraan Waali Gali was in one team and everyone from Model Town was in the other team. Inter-gali matches were more competitive than intra-gali ones. They were also mostly dominated by older children and played with a leather ball instead of rubber or a plastic ball.

OK, so you have the players now. What else do you need? A bat and a ball. Wickets were good to have, though at most times wickets were made using whatever was available. It could be a wall with three lines drawn with chalk or coal, or bricks heaped on top of each other (which were difficult to assemble again if an overzealous wicket-keeper attempted a forceful stumping), or some plastic pipes lying around or even a scooter with its *stepney* (spare tyre) serving as a wicket.

The toss between the two captains would happen either with a coin or rolling the bat in hand or some sort of a local technique. Which player would bat first? That again would depend on the criteria used by Sumit Bhaiya to select the team.

Cricket balls are like thoughts. You can't control them. Fly they will. But there are penalties to pay in this world if you go too far. So, if you were playing in your house compound and hit the ball into a neighbour's house, you were out.

You were also out if the ball went to any house if you were playing on the street. Which to you as the batsman did not feel fair because you probably would have hit your best shot ever, which in an open ground would have been a definite six.

However, the rule was probably justified because someone will now have to work their magic to fetch the ball back. This task usually landed on the shoulders of the batsman. The rules of karma were clear – you hit it, you fetch it.

"Auntyji, *woh* actually our ball went into your house."

"Why do you have to play all the time? *Saara din time waisht, saara din.* Waste your time all day. Don't even let us sleep in the afternoon."

"Sorry, Auntyji."

"And why don't you make Monu play with you? Monu, come here, get the ball, and if you don't play with them from tomorrow, then see. Always sitting at home, wasting time. *Saara din time waisht, saara din.*"

"*Hanji* Auntyji. Thank you, Auntyji. Monu, *kal aa jana fir.* Join us tomorrow."

Triumphant return with the ball. This is how young brains learnt negotiation skills.

Trying to get the ball back from someone's grandmother could be even more difficult.

Imagine if the ball went to the same house again. The match would be abandoned at that point. "*Chalo yar, kal sahi ab.*" Oh well, let's play tomorrow then.

Gali mohalla matches could be limited to 5 or 6 overs per team. Which meant each batsman was allowed to play a few balls, usually the maximum of 6 balls (that is, an over). The batsman could come back later in the innings if all other batsmen were out.

The same rationing was implemented for bowling. However, some magnanimous players such as yours truly would completely forgo their bowling quota for others. There was a reason for that, a wide one too. As Joshi, my friend with knowledge of all sports in the world would say, "*Dhawan, you should bowl from the spare wicket. Only then your ball will land in front of the batsman."* What could I do? The balls I bowled ended up being wide – all of them.

My best skills were in fielding. I had quick reflexes and could anticipate the trajectory of a ball. If I were a batsman, I would probably be Rahul Dravid. At times I would be Tendulkar. I would probably be Kumble when balling. Spin would have been my forte. Plus, I would have been good at keeping wickets.

And why wouldn't I be? Every child growing up in India would have donned the India cap at some point in their dream world. Every one of us has had an international career playing in blue.

When you start growing up you start seeing individual personalities become prominent during playing. During college days, Joshi, for instance, would bat with an expression as if the whole world was in danger and he was the sole saviour.

Madan Gopal or MG on the other hand was Mr Cool. He would play in his pyjamas, chappals and half-sleeve vests. He had a good technique for batting and bowling.

Somesh Kumar, who wanted to join the army but ended up studying computers with us, would prepare well for a match, be dressed for the occasion, perfect his stance, play the first 5 balls in the over without scoring any runs and get out at the last ball.

Pushappreet Singh, our tall, lanky friend, 6 feet 5 inches, scared opponents just by his turbo-charged bowling run-up.

Gurminder Singh, or Gora, our well-built and soft-spoken friend once left the whole opposition team in college shivering with fear when he was wrongly given out. Out came all the wickets in one go as Gora pulled them apart and roared, like Sunny Deol of *Gadar* (2001).

Jassu played proper gentlemen cricket, with all his cricketing gear and whites. No wonder he once told me that a shirt does not go with a pyjama. *Thank you, Jassu. See, I remembered it.*

Life has taken over since as all of us search our own paths. You miss the time spent with friends. You reminisce the joy of playing uninhibited. You smile.

Right, what's next.

9.

Passport-Size Photo

*N*arcissism comes in many different sizes. I can't remember how many times I have seen my face, in passport size. What could you do? Nothing happened without a passport-size photo. You owed your identity to a passport-size photo. I have a passport-size photo, therefore I am.

Among all the photo sizes (4 x 6, postcard, among others), the passport size has attained the status of a king. Machiavelli said that it is better to be feared than loved if one cannot be both. That's the passport-size photo for you. With fear, it rules.

Any identity document issued by the government – be it a driving licence, a ration card, or (surprise, surprise) a passport – requires your passport-size photo. So does college or university admission forms or application forms for various professional entrance exams.

The first time I needed a passport-size photo was for the class 10 exams. I was in Dasmesh Public School, Faridkot at that time, 16 years of age. The passport-size photo I got clicked was in my school uniform, white shirt, blue striped tie, and blue blazer, adorned with a teen moustache.

I looked pretty serious in that photo, maybe due to the pressure of the class 10 board exams, or as a result of getting photographed for a passport-size photo for the first time. The photo was used in my identity card for admission to the examination hall. The identity card remains with me to date.

After I had finished class 10, we moved to Chandigarh and used the same photo for my admission in class 11. I didn't like my new school. Perhaps because of moving to a new city and a new school with new classmates, made worse by the pressure of private tuitions, rat race, expectations.

Prompted by my adolescent self I joined a gym in class 11. 'Prime Bodies' as it was called, in Sector 32 in Chandigarh. There was a photo studio in the same market. That shop was to become my primary source of photos for the next few years.

I had a new passport photo clicked that year, which was used in my Prime Bodies ID card. That was me with my printed, tight-hugging T-shirt, and the face of a growing-yet-thinking-he-is-grown-up 17-year-old boy.

This was the time when my fondness for *khadi kurtas* had taken firm root. I have loved wearing khadi. It's natural, it's hand-woven, it's cotton (well, it can also be silk or wool but I have liked cotton). Cool in summers, warm in winters. You can get traditional kurtas or other ethnic wear as well as more trendy garments in khadi.

I bought a few kurtas from the Khadi Udyog and the Fab India shops. One of my passport-size photos from that time has me wearing a khadi kurta along with a sleeveless khadi jacket and supporting a light French beard. I didn't need that photo. It was just a guilty pleasure.

I had moved to college around the time when the *Hindustan Times* (*HT*) launched an 'HT Privileged Citizen' card. The card was supposed to give you discounts at some shops. I applied for it. You just had to fill a form, giving your contact details and a passport-size photo. I used my khadi kurta photo, which I thought went well with the newspaper theme as journalists and writers were always shown wearing kurtas on TV. I received the card by post and, and lo and behold, became a privileged citizen.

I did try to use the card once at a toll tax collection barrier. Dad and I were travelling to Delhi in a taxi and there was a toll tax barrier near Karnal in the state of Haryana. The toll tax was newly introduced at that time and people were reluctant to cough up money for just passing through a road.

The taxi driver asked for the payment, unless, he said, you have any privilege to pass. I thought why not try my Privileged Citizen card. I always carried it in my wallet, just in case. The barrierwaala who was manning the barrier looked at the card, looked at me and said that this would not work. So we had to shell out the money. I never had the pleasure to use the card, ever. But it remains a part of my paraphernalia of growing up.

When you are in college you start inventing reasons to go out with friends and have a party. Two of them were due to my facial hair, resulting in more photos.

My moustache was taking a long time to join my beard, to make a complete French beard. There was a small gap – the 'bridge' was not complete yet. I had promised my friends that the day the gap closed, I would give them a party. That day arrived after a year or so, and I was only too eager to throw a party, provided photos were clicked to mark the special achievement. That request was duly obliged.

On another occasion in college, it was decided that I should get a photo with a turban. I had not tied a turban before. Except once in a school play when I'd played the role of a Punjabi teacher. The thing with a turban is that it looks good only with a full-grown beard. French cut or stubble won't do. Therefore, I grew my beard for 3 months. *Growing a beard is like raising a teenager. Terrible until it matures up.*

On the appointed day, all my friends from college gathered at one of our class fellows' place, after attending our classes. Those who knew how to tie a turban tied it on my head. We went to a photo studio and had my photo clicked – in passport size. We then went to 'Sindhi Sweets' and had some hearty *chhole bhature* (deep-fried leavened bread, served with chickpea curry).

Passport-size photos were printed in multiples of four – either 4 or 8 or 12. I would ask the photographers for the negatives, in case I needed to develop the photos again. Most photographers were fine with that. However, some of them introduced a new policy to keep the negatives with them so that the customers would have to come back every time they needed more copies. I did not like that. It was my photo, my negative, my personal property.

Application forms needing passport-size photos came with their own set of guidelines: the photo should be taken only against a white background, and no smiling, please. The *not smiling* one was a difficult one to get accustomed too. Throughout your childhood you are taught to smile at the camera. And now suddenly the government changes the rules as you step out of childhood. Not fair.

I think the government must have also made another rule – no expressions allowed on the photographer's face. A person is sitting in front of you, on a low-quality, cold, metallic stool that you have, curbing his smile, keeping eyes open, trying hard not to blink, trying hard not to look at your studio umbrellas, keeping his neck in a strange sideways tilt and chin artificially facing upwards, on a momentous occasion of getting himself photographed for the mighty passport-size photo, and you, you sir have no expression at all on your face. Absolutely nothing. How cruel.

Some photographers had started to add a bit of glam to the process by keeping a tie (already knotted), and a comb in addition to a mirror. I'll bring my own matching tie, thank you very much. And using someone else's comb was a complete no-no. My dad had a habit of keeping a small comb in his pocket all the time. I grew up thinking that it was a normal thing to do. So I used to keep a comb with me in my trouser pocket wherever I went, until recently.

My dad was also keen on his passport-size photos, perhaps more than I was. All his photographs have always been formal, all tie and suit. Maybe it was because getting photographed was a celebration in its own right. Before the advent of digital cameras and mobile phones, photographs were taken almost always on special occasions. People would go to photo studios to get photographed. Albums were made using printed photos. Photos which you went back to and looked at with fondness, again and again. Annual family photos were commonplace in those days.

Dad had a dear friend in Ferozepur whom we addressed as *Chachaji* (father's younger brother). Chachaji's brother had a photo studio in the town where dad, mom, my sister and I went once a year for our family photo. Our photographs were black and white to start with, turning into coloured ones as the years progressed.

Did I tell you that few questions have perplexed me in life more than 'gloss or matt'? I faced exceptional difficulty understanding and remembering which was which. So let's write it down. Gloss is natural, looks better, but can be spoiled by fingerprints. Whereas matt is shiny and scaled, does not get easily spoiled by fingerprints, and is disliked by me.

If you have used glue to affix a passport-size photo on an application form, you will know that it leaves unintended marks on the paper. Plus, it can damage the photo and leave your hands sticky and gluey. Therefore, Fevistick was a welcome addition to the arsenal of an applicant (to anything) in India at that time. You just rolled the stick at the back of the photo and fixed the photo on the 'upper right-hand corner' of the form.

However, you had to be careful that you held the photo by its edges, else you risked leaving your fingerprints on the photo. And you should never, ever, do that or else you might upset the *babu* (government officer) who received your application form. So, you took a hand towel or a handkerchief and wiped off any fingerprints or extra Fevistick on and around the photo.

And never staple a photo to the application form. The form was super sensitive – it did not like being pricked and certainly did not believe in acupuncture. Sometimes you were asked to enclose 2 or 3 copies of your passport-size photo along with the application form, with strict instructions to "enclose and not affix". The best way to do that was using paper clips. If you used something like paper pins, that ruined the photo as well as the form.

The more sophisticated the reason for using a passport-size photo, the more embellished was the process of using it. If you were applying for just any odd 'job-shob', you were simply asked to affix a photo and that was it.

On the other hand, if you had finally reached the status of applying for your passport, you had to certify that it was in fact your photo, a true likeness of you, which was not more than 6 months old, and that you were in your *poore hosho-hawaas* (in full possession of your senses) when you applied for it and did it according to your own will, without coercion.

You had to write your name and date of birth at the back of the photo. But you had to make sure that you didn't apply unnecessary pressure else your handwriting would be engraved on your nose or lips on the other side.

You also had to make sure that the ink dried out quickly, else it would ruin the photo – so no ink pens or even Pilot pens.

Ball-point pens were the best bet. But only black ink was allowed. Some considerate *daftars* (government offices) allowed blue as well. But that's it. And everything had to be written in CAPS.

Some daftars required you to sign across the photo. This would put me in a fix. Should I start my signature from the application form and end up on the photo? Or start from the photo and end up on the form? In any case, you had to make sure that your signature did not end up on your face. Using a passport-size photo was not child's play.

Passport-size photos revealed their supremacy when *phoren* lands beckoned. I witnessed this first hand when I helped my friend Goldy in applying for a visa to Canada.

I met Goldy in college and he became a good friend. His understanding of society and economy was advanced for his age. *I find it intriguing how Western female names (Goldy, Vicky, Honey, among others) ended up as male names in India, especially common in the northern states (Punjab/Haryana/Delhi).*

Where were we? Ah yes, so Goldy and I did many rounds on his scooter to various offices to get his visa documents ready.

It was a trend in Chandigarh those days that dashing *munde* (boys) do not wear a helmet or have *stepney* (a spare tyre) at the back of their scooter. It must have looked a bit odd seeing Goldy driving the scooter without wearing his helmet and I wearing my 'street hawk' helmet on the pillion. I could also not remove stepney from my scooter for the fear of being stuck somewhere if a tyre was punctured. Why would girls object to a spare tyre, I used to wonder.

Did you know the origin of the word 'stepney'? I used to think that it was some variant of the word 'step'. But that's not the case. Apparently, the word comes from the name of the first company to manufacture spare tyres "Stepney Iron Mongers", which was located in Stepney Street in Llanelli in Wales (UK).

Goldy and I visited the local courts a few times to get his photos and documents attested. The court complexes were one of the most esoteric places you could think of. Nobody seemed to know what was going on, but then everybody sort of did. Sometimes it seemed the other way around.

There were a large number of desks in the open with 'Notary Public' displayed proudly on sign boards in front of them. The desks would be surrounded by many individuals, some sitting, some standing, some jumping or peeping to find out which deity was seated in the middle. It was none other than notaryji, adorning black suit and white shirt. He was the one who would attest your documents. He was the main man. And there were a large number of main men in the court complex.

There was no manual, no guidance on how to deal with this aspect of life. You had to venture out, learn quickly and improvise. The first thing to do was to pick one of the notaries and tell them that you wanted to get documents attested for a visa. Someone would tell you, without looking at you, that you first had to get an affidavit, for which you would need to get a stamp (pronounced as *staam* or *ishtaam*) paper for Rs 10, or Rs 20, or other denominations.

Now you would have to find out where to get the stamp paper. You were directed to another desk or a window where someone was selling stamp papers to what seemed like the whole city. As there was no queue or any token system, you just had to force your hand through the sea of people, clutching in it the money equal to the denomination of the stamp paper you wanted, towards the seller.

Once you 'felt' that the cash had been removed from your hand, you forced your head, and if lucky, the rest of the body in the direction of your hand. You were handed a pen to scribble your name, your father's name and address on a large register and the stamp paper was handed to you. You then wriggled your way out of the crowd, body first, then head and then your hand. The next task was to find a typist who could prepare an affidavit. Typists in those days had vintage mechanical typewriters. The rhythmic tick-tick of the keys hitting the drums could be heard all over the court building. I used to enjoy the rhythm.

Spelling mistakes were common but we were told that spelling didn't matter, you just had to get your name, address and your father's name correct. The document was now ready to go to the notary public for signature.

You would now give all documents and photos to the notary's assistant who would put three or four stamps on each document. You could hardly make out what each stamp meant. It all read blue. If the documents were meant for a visa, there was an extra stamp for that – "valid for embassy" – in red. This stamp cost almost double the rest of the stamps. You had to negotiate in advance how much the stamping and signing would cost.

The assistant then handed documents to the notary for final signature. *"Aa jra ghugghi maar deo."* This is how the assistant requested the notary to get his signature. It's an expression used in Punjabi if you want to ask someone to sign but giving them the impression that this action should hardly require any effort on their part, and they don't need to read it before signing.

Finally, Goldy's documents were ready.

I had my share of visits to administrative offices when I applied for my driving licence in Chandigarh. It was exciting. Any identity document issued in Chandigarh was deemed to be worth more compared to the states of Punjab or Haryana.

Chandigarh, a union territory, is the capital city of the two states of Punjab and Haryana. It came into existence in 1952, one of the first planned cities of independent India. Its architecture, designed by Swiss–French architect Le Corbusier, is acclaimed internationally.

Getting a learner's licence was easy. You filled a form with your passport-size photo, submitted it at the 'estate office' along with the rest of the documents, and you were issued a learner's licence. There were many agents who offered their services to those standing in queue to submit driving licence applications. Many succumbed. I managed to hold on to my file and submitted it on my own.

I then applied for the full licence. I was nervous on the day of the driving test. I went to the test centre and was asked to drive my car. "*Aathaa bana deo*" (Make an 8), I was asked. And that's it. You can make an 8 with your car, you know to drive safely.

At that time the Chandigarh administration had started a new initiative. They replaced paper licences with smart cards. My photo was clicked at the estate office and the photo was engrossed on the smart card. This was a pleasant experience and outcome for me. Things were changing, for the better.

Then the day finally arrived when I got a new passport-size photo for my passport. In those days you reached the pinnacle of your love affair with passport-size photos when your passport was made. You were finally there in life.

10.

Kite Flying

Kite flying has been passed down from generation to generation as a traditional sport. It is much loved in parts of India and Pakistan, and a lovely example of the shared culture despite all the differences between the two neighbours. My early childhood, spent in Ferozepur, a town in Punjab which borders Pakistan, is filled with memories of flying kites, called *patang* in Hindi or *guddi* in Punjabi.

The kite flying season starts around October when the winters are about to arrive in north India. This used to be the time to buy new kites or start using the ones saved from the last season. In those days you could buy normal kites for 25 paise and special, large ones for 50 paise or one rupee.

The line or string used for flying kites, *dora* (or *manja*) as we called it, also came in different varieties. The thinner dora was sharp and came in dark colours – black, brown or dark green. The thicker variety was not as sharp and usually came in lighter, fancier colours – pink and orange, among others.

Dora contained crushed glass – that's what made it sharp. Getting cuts on hands while flying was normal. People carried on regardless; some used bandages, some did not bother at all.

Dora was available in three different shapes, depending on

the length of the string. The shortest piece of dora came bundled in the shape of an 8. You had to wind the dora on the palm of your hand, using your thumb and little finger, to get that shape.

A somewhat longer string of dora was rolled onto a ball of paper (called *gola*). The extra-long strings of dora were available on a wooden spool, called a *firki* or *charkhi* (*charrakhri* in Punjabi – a bit convoluted to spell it in English). The spool had two small wooden rods on either end. You could use a stand to hold the charrakhri, though most people just let it roll on the floor while flying or another person would hold it for the kite flyer.

When you were done flying a kite, a charrakhri was the easiest to wind up. Rest one rod on the inside of your elbow and rotate the other rod backwards with the other hand.

Wounding it back on the round gola was not difficult, except that if you wound it loose, it could come off.

A small piece of dora could be wound back in the shape of an 8 on your hand.

Huge amount of dora went waste in the end as it got entangled and you could spend hours opening the knots. Which reminds me of these words from the qawwali sung by Nusrat Fateh Ali Khan '*Tum ik gorakh dhandha ho*' (adapted from Niaz Khialvi's poem with the same title).

Falsafi ko behas ke andar khuda milta nahi,
Dor ko suljha raha hai aur sira milta nahi.
Akal mein jo ghir gya, woh la-inteha kyun kar hua,
Jo samajh mein aa gya, fir woh khuda kyun kar hua.

(You won't find the almighty in philosophical arguments.
It's like trying to untie the knots of a string but struggling to find its ends.

How can the infinite be bound by the realms of logic?
If it could be understood, how could that be called almighty?)

This qawwali features poetry of the highest order, and music bordering on ecstasy. Highly recommended.

Kites have to be harnessed before you can fly them. Harnessing kites is quite a skill which you learn by practice. How a kite flies and 'fights' depends on the harness to a great extent. The harness is made using a short string of dora tied to the frame of a kite. The frame is made of two thin wooden sticks (or it was in those days), which intersect each other in the shape of an arched bow holding an arrow.

The intersection of the two sticks is used to tie one end of the harness and the lower part of the 'arrow' to tie the other end. The dora is then tied to the harness and the kite is ready to fly. You could lift the kite off the ground on your own. But if someone could hold the kite for you at that point, it made the lift-off easier.

Once airborne, kites fly higher when you give them a short pull (called a *tunka* in Punjabi) and then release the dora. The alternating sequence of pulls and releases is more frequent to start with, becoming more stable as the kite reaches some height.

You do not want it to be windy, else you won't be able to control the kite. A gentle breeze is perfect. Flying a kite is like rearing a baby. You give them an initial lift-off, you steer them as far as you can, and when the time comes, they have to start fighting their own battles.

Once your kite is flying among other kites, battles happen. There will be victories and there will be losses. We called a kite battle a *pecha*. Dora of two kites lock horns and the battle begins. The kite with the sharper and stronger dora, and a skilful flyer, would normally win.

Sometimes a pecha would go on for hours as neither of the two flyers would strike first. They would keep releasing their dora, a few centimetres at a time because they knew that the one who pulled back their dora first will most likely lose. That is why you needed plenty of dora.

The players couldn't normally see each other. They could see just their kites locked in the air. It was an anonymous battle.

It was difficult to call a draw even if the kite flyers intended. Once a pecha happens, you have to fight. Unless it is getting late in the evening and you hear your mom commanding you to stop wasting your time. In which case you pull your dora and lose the battle in the skies to survive the more ominous one on the ground.

All houses had rooftops. There were no apartments, no balconies. Kites were flown on rooftops. We had two rooftops in our ancestral house – one at the front of the house and one at the rear. Which meant I could go from one rooftop to another depending on the wind direction. Not that it made any difference. I hardly won. What can I say – our house was surrounded by expert flyers, and I was just a kid and that too a peace-loving one.

When someone loses a kite, someone else gets to win it. Sometimes the victor would capture the losing kite in-air, using their own kite, and bring it back as a trophy. This was the ultimate victory and a rare one.

More often than not the kites had to be caught by hand to be won. Sometimes it was easy. You caught hold of the dora of a free-flying kite passing through your rooftop and pulled it back on the ground. But sometimes kites would get caught in TV antennae. You would have to be lucky to reach it in the first place. And if you did, even luckier to get it out in one piece.

Kites in our street had the habit of landing onto a neighbour's house which had a large rooftop. It was of no use to them as they did not fly kites. They were not friendly either, which meant we could not ask them for the kites.

But you cannot just watch kites lying unused, not getting their due attention. Something had to be done. So, we used to try to tow them back to us using a stone or a small piece of wood tied to a string. Bringing back a kite in this way felt like an incredible achievement, nothing short of a bank heist.

Trouble brewed when there were multiple claimants. It came down to hand-to-hand combat. The unspoken code was that whatever happens, the kite shalt not be harmed. That would be sacrilege. Noses, shirts, groins, all could be brought in the line of fire, but not the kite.

While I was not the one to get involved in such scuffles, one incident forced me into a bit of a clash.

I was about 10 years of age at that time. Our street was a cul-de-sac, and at the end of the street was a stable for horses (called *ahaata*). In those days, horses were mainly deployed to pull passenger tongas in Ferozepur city. We just happened to have horses as our neighbours.

One day a lost kite was hovering over our street and there were two of us out there to get it. We could see that it would land in the ahaata. We ran towards its rooftop.

This was not advisable as the horses could come running in or out of the ahaata at any time. One of my cousins had previously been hit by a horse in our street and had to get stitches on his forehead.

Anyways, we were up there on the rooftop. The kite was dropping slowly. Suddenly I felt as if someone pushed me from behind.

I fell from the rooftop onto the floor of the ahaata. I became unconscious. The next thing I remember is seeing mom's face. She looked frightened. She was trying to get me out of the ahaata but I was unable to walk. It felt like I was carrying a huge weight on my back. Mom picked me up and carried me home.

I was lucky that day. The ground where I fell had stacks of bricks for the construction that was going on in the ahaata. But the spot where I fell, just that exact spot, was free of bricks. It was plain, soft ground.

I will be honest with you; I am not sure to this day if I was pushed by the other guy or I jumped on my own to catch the kite. I have tried to run the sequence of events over and over in my head but haven't been able to get a definite answer.

One nice thing that the other guy did was to inform my mom. Otherwise, I may not have been found for long, or found by the horses first.

This is what kites do to you. I was taken to the hospital, to a bone specialist. His name has somehow remained stuck in my memory. Dr Kamalkant. I had a fracture on both feet. Well, not exactly a fracture – some tear in the ligament. My feet were all tied up in bandages and I was on bed rest for the next two weeks.

I would soak my feet in warm water mixed with salt every night before sleep and re-bandage them after applying Iodex balm. I wonder what my parents would have gone through. It was merely a kite.

Those couple of weeks resulted in two experiences, one of which had a lasting impact. One of Bauji's (my grandad's) devotees was lovingly known as Maaji, an old lady, who visited our home frequently. When she saw me in bandages, she handed me her *dholki* drum, which she used to play during *kirtans* (devotional singing, usually in a group).

That turned out to be a perfect gift. Sitting on a *manji* (Punjabi word for a jute woven cot, also called *chaarpai* in Hindi) in open air, I started playing dholki, enjoyed it and realised my love for music, percussion and singing, which carries on till date.

The second experience related to my bedrest caused a bit of disappointment for me at that time. One of my *mamaji's* family came to visit us. They, along with my sister and dad, went to visit the border that separates India and Pakistan close to our town. I was not in a position to go and mom stayed back to look after me.

It was to take me nearly three decades to finally visit the border. It is called the Hussainiwala border, located in the vicinity of the martyrdom place of the freedom fighters Bhagat Singh, Rajguru and Sukhdev.

That visit was worth the wait. The one-upmanship and thumping of boots from the two sides, the flag-lowering ceremony and closing of gates and the patriotic zeal from both the countries were not less than any Bollywood movie. The thing that struck me the most was seeing how close Pakistan was. Its roads, its people, its culture, all were there to be seen, first time in real.

The highlight of the kite flying season was Basant Panchami, the day to celebrate the arrival of spring season. The festival was held normally in late January or February.

"Aayi Basant, paala udant", people would say (arrival of spring makes winter disappear).

Basant Panchami was the culmination of the kite flying season and was celebrated with enthusiasm. Yellow was the theme of the day. People wore yellow clothes, and sweet, yellow rice (with *kesar* – saffron) or *chana daal khichdi* (mix of rice and split chickpea lentils) was prepared at home.

The preparation for Basant used to start a few months earlier. People would save the best kites they had won for Basant. I kept them under my bed.

A few days leading to Basant, shops were full of kites. I would buy two or three different sizes of kites, along with new dora. Band-Aid was also an essential buy for me as cuts on hands were expected.

On the day of the Basant festival, kites would start appearing in the sky early in the morning and by 10 am the sky was full of kites – all different colours, shapes and sizes. All flown by people of all ages, skills and resources. Rooftops became the most happening places.

Music cassettes were played on rooftops using big loudspeakers. This was accompanied by chatting, eating and arguing. Kite flying meanwhile carried on with full zeal. Quick lunch breaks were taken; snacking kept you going. There were peanuts and *gur* (jaggery) or *mooli* (radish) cut in 4 petals, sprinkled with black salt.

Action happened all over the sky. Kites were won and lost. There was fun, excitement, pain.

No Basant festival was complete without this Punjabi song by Mahendra Kapoor floating in the air, along with kites:

Tu patlo jehi ik guddi ein,
Te hawa ch firdi uddi ein,
Mere hatthan wich e dor teri
Mann kehna yaar da...
Jee karda hai tenu maar dyaan
Ik tunka pyar da
Ho tunka pyar da ...

(In brief, this is an upbeat song that uses kite flying as a metaphor for romantic entanglement.)

The last kites were flown as the day ended. I flew my best kite at the end, a grand finale to the day. When it was completely dark, some fellas with undying spirit flew small lanterns attached to kites. You could see just flames meandering in the sky. It brought a serene, almost meditative end to the day and to the kite flying season. *Om tat sat.*

11.

Street Food

*T*he idea called India is not complete without mixing street food in its recipe. Street food in India is as diverse as the country. As you read this chapter, you may feel not much has changed over the years. The same street food continues to be in favour. Which is true. However, new cuisines have been added, as have new reasons for enjoying street food. Marketing of street food has become more prominent. But yes, a few things are still the same, including the joy of street food.

The first thing that comes to mind when talking about street food is *golgappa* or *paani poori*. The name varies by different regions in the country, but basically, they are small, round, hollow, crispy puff-pastries, often filled with small chunks of boiled potatoes, chickpeas, and tamarind chutney, accompanied by spicy *paani* (water). Every town has well-known paani poori joints. People standing around a *rehri* (a small cart) or a stall, swallowing golgappas and sipping spiced water is a common sight; quintessentially Indian.

The *golgappewaalas* (those who serve golgappas) have an excellent working memory. They seem to remember, without any effort, how many golgappas per plate are remaining for everyone being served at a time.

The *paani* that comes with golgappas makes all the difference. Spicy, tangy water, mixed with different spices and chutneys (*imli*: tamarind, *pudina*: mint, among others), poured into a golgappa is a mouth-watering mix.

The spicy paani has always been in high demand. We would ask for more and more of it after eating our plate of golgappas. Spicy paani proved to be a saviour once. I had choked on a golgappa. A small piece of golgappa got stuck and I could not breathe. One of my cousins, who was with me at that time, gave me a first-class tip. Drink small sips of paani that you are having and swallow gently. It did the trick, and works every time.

Next in line in the hierarchy of street food is *papri* chaat. The main ingredients are papri (crispy, fried crackers), small chunks of boiled potatoes, yoghurt and tamarind chutney. Sometimes it is also garnished with *bhujia* (dry, deep-fried crispy snack, usually made from chickpea flour), coriander leaves, or pomegranate seeds. You would also get *dahi vada or dahi bhalla* (deep-fried lentil fritters) at the same shop. Paapri is replaced with fritters, the rest of the ingredients usually remain the same.

Different flavours of chutney are used by different *chaatwaalas* (those who sell chaat). Some generous ones garnish the chaat with *kishmish* (raisins) or *kaju* (cashew nuts). Now that you are in this shop, why not have a *tikki* as well – the aaloo tikki. Potato patty fried on a hot plate, served with chopped raw onion, grated radish, yoghurt, green chillies, ginger, and different chutneys. Yum.

Have you tried sweet *petha*? It is sugary, chewy candy made from ash gourd (also called winter melon). Petha made in Agra has a special status. Let me tell you about a petha-related incident from my childhood.

A hawker would visit our neighbourhood selling sweet petha. And, I liked it. One afternoon I went out hearing the hawker's call. He was standing in our street and I was the sole customer. I bought a few pieces of petha and was taking them back home in a small paper bag when three large dogs gathered around me. They were staring at me, ears upright, canine teeth shining bright. I witnessed fear that day. I was 6.

I started running towards home. The dogs started running after me. There are some races you know you can't win. I threw the pieces of petha towards them. That made them busy for a few seconds, which was just the amount of time I needed to reach home, open the door, and never want to open it again. I was both hounded and saved by petha that day. The fear of canines lingers on.

One thing I miss about childhood is going out for a walk after dinner. Mom, dad, my sister and I would go for a stroll every evening. During summers this was the only time in the day when the weather was comfortable enough to go out and enjoy the cool breeze.

The *karyana* shops (local, family-owned, grocery stores) remained open till late and we would buy one or two items of grocery during our walk. At times we would stop by the rehris selling *falooda* or *matka kulfi*. The creamy ice cream in terracotta tumblers was served with *falooda seviyan* (dessert noodles similar to vermicelli), garnished with Rooh Afza sharbat. The perfect end to the day.

Rehris selling platters of cut fruit were a common sight, especially during summer. You could get pieces of fruits such as melon, watermelon, sugarcane and papaya, sprinkled with black pepper and black salt. I don't think I ever had any cut fruit from rehris. It was not considered healthy. There was dust and heat, not to mention flies hovering around.

The best noodles are made in India. Chinese noodles cooked Indian style. I don't think India has adopted any other foreign cuisine as widely as Chinese. I wonder how noodles became commonplace in India. When were they introduced in India? Who brought them across the border?

Shock fry some cabbage and onions in a wok, in goes the noodles and salt, spices and soya sauce. That's it. Enjoy it with some chilli sauce. There were shops and rehris everywhere selling noodles, including at weekly *sabzi mandis* (farmer markets).

Another delicious fusion of Chinese and Indian food is Veg Manchurian – deep-fried vegetable dumplings dipped in thick, sweet and sour gravy.

If you are in Chandigarh, don't miss Chinese noodles in the market of Sector 34. The shops in the area would give large portions; one plate was sufficient for 2 or 3 people.

Now that you are in Sector 34, why not try another remarkable food that India has adopted – cake. It looks like the first bakery in India was established in the early 1880s, in Thalassery (Kerala).

Cakes made in India are soft, creamy and fluffy. Fresh pastries melt in the mouth, literally. Pineapple pastry was the most favoured pastry when we were growing up, later joined by black forest. Birthday cakes were made to order, in kilograms. Bakeries handed out a slip of paper to write the message that you wanted to appear on the cake. Happy birthday, xyz. And their age in numbers.

Birthday parties were incomplete without cakes. There was something uniquely Indian about the birthday parties during my childhood. The ritual was well known. Candles were put on the cake, one more than the age of the birthday girl or boy. The cake was placed on the dining table, surrounded by everyone invited – and you would have invited every child you knew.

You would blow all the candles except one. Mom shall take away the lighted candle to the kitchen so that it remains safe and lit for as long as possible, which was considered good luck.

You would cut the cake with a knife, which had a red ribbon tied to it. Everyone clapped for you and sang happy birthday. Photographers were hired to capture the moments.

The first piece of cake was put into the mouth of the birthday girl/boy who then gave the second piece to someone close to them, usually a sibling or a parent. Mom would cut the cake into small pieces. Some adults would smear someone's face with cake. Wonderful.

Grown-ups avoided alcohol during birthday parties of children. If they did have it, the glasses were covered with white napkins as a social courtesy, a tradition still followed at some family gatherings, especially weddings.

You were given a cake piece along with a gulab jamun dipped in sweet syrup, a samosa, a *pakorra* (deep-fried battered vegetables) with chutney and a biscuit. All in one go, all in one plate, which was made of paper. So most of the cake pieces I have eaten have been chutney flavoured. But hey ho – it's happy, happy birthday and time for presents.

If it was your birthday, the best time of the day was when everyone had left and you could open the presents. One by one, rescuing the wrapper where you could, disregarding it where you could not, you opened every gift with anticipation and delight.

When you are in college, you don't need to wait for birthdays. Every afternoon becomes a celebration. We would have samosas or bread pakorras at our college canteen for lunch, or potato croquette on special days. And masala chai. With friends.

For dessert, we would have cream rolls – puff-pastry rolls filled with whipped cream. We were on first-name terms with the canteen *thekedaar* (contractor). This meant that we would get fresh samosas, hot from the frying pan, not the ones that were made like 2 minutes ago.

During my college days, 'patties' became the in thing. These were triangle-shaped puff-pastry filled with potato or paneer filling. Our canteen thekedaar did not stock them. So I would visit Sector 44 market in Chandigarh with Bhatnagar and other friends after college to have patties and coffee. The shops there had heated units with a glass window to display the patties and keep them warm.

Coffee was made using espresso machines. Patties were served in disposable paper plates with ketchup, and coffee in small disposable cups. I loved the chocolate powder sprinkled on my coffee. Perfect in winters.

Nowadays, rehris selling *paav bhaji* are a commonplace. Thick curry made of mashed vegetables served with a soft bread roll. It wasn't as readily available when I was growing up, where I was growing up.

Another snack in vogue these days is sweetcorn kernels mixed with spices, served in a plastic cup. During my childhood, whole sweetcorn (or *chhalli*) rubbed with lemon and spices was a common snack. But I find it easier to eat sweetcorn kernels in a cup – easy on the teeth and you can mix the spices better.

Sector 17 plaza was the most sought-after shopping hub in Chandigarh. It has served as a favourite rendezvous for guys and gals over the years. It has also served a variety of street food to those guys and gals. *Bhelpuri* has been one of them. Get some puffed rice, mix small pieces of boiled potatoes and other vegetables, and add some herbs and spices. Don't forget some tamarind chutney and lemon juice. I have tried it a couple of times in Sector 17 (the bhelpuri I mean). It's hot. Go ahead, enjoy it.

'Softy' or soft ice cream in a cone has also held its place as street food over the years. Vanilla and strawberry were the sole flavours for a long time. Nowadays you can get chocolate, butterscotch, and many other flavours. How good is the softy is determined not just by its flavour but also by its consistency. It should be soft enough to fill the cone to the very bottom. And the lower part of the cone should be wrapped in tissue paper, to avoid soiling your hands as the softy will melt.

Would you consider popcorn as street food? It's available in Sector 17, not far from the softy corner, just in case you happen to be there.

How about *paranthaas*? Unleavened flatbread, made with wheat flour. Would you consider paranthaas as street food? If you are in Delhi, you probably will. I stayed in Delhi for a couple of months looking for a job along with my friend Joshi. A number of our meals were paranthaas from a rehri. Hot paranthaas with butter on top and dahi (curd or yoghurt) and *achaar* (pickle). You could choose between aaloo or *gobi* options (paranthaas filled with potato or cauliflower mix). Who cared how healthy they were and what calorie count they had.

I have many childhood memories with *kulche chhole*. There was a famous shop in Ferozepur at a place named 'Choohi Chowk' that sold kulche chhole. Spicy chhole (chickpea curry) was served with a soft flatbread (kulche) or rice. Chickpeas were garnished with onion and green chillies. They had a small shop, with large metallic pateelas or pans, one for holding chhole and one for rice.

Let me use this opportunity to give you one tip. Never have hot tea straight after eating spicy kulche chhole. It burns your tongue by a factor of 10.

There was another vendor in Ferozepur who sold kulche chhole. He would sit outside his house at 2 pm every day with freshly made chhole in a big, metallic pateela. When you asked for chhole, he would slide the lid from the pateela, just enough to put a ladle to get chhole out. His stock would be over by 3 pm. Everything sold in an hour.

Kulche chhole could also be had outside our school. Kulchaas were cut in two halves and stuffed with dry chhole, mixed with spices and onion. One stuffed kulchaa cost Rs 2.

Chhole bhature is another sumptuous meal. The most in-demand shop to get these in Chandigarh was, and probably still is, Sindhi Sweets in Sector 17. This was the most desirable item on their menu and had the shortest serving time. In one plate they served two large, freshly made bhatura breads, two *sabzis* (vegetable curries) – chhole and aaloo, accompanied with onion and achaar. If this is not heavy enough for you, why not also have a large glass of sweet *lassi* (yoghurt drink) at the shop.

Dosa may not qualify as street food but I will write about it because I like dosas (thin, savoury pancakes or crepes made with battered rice and lentils). At times Datta and I visited the Indian Coffee House in Sector 17 in Chandigarh. The restaurant still has an old-world charm. Hardly anything ever changes at that place, which made it even more special.

It retains its traditional ambience and is filled with nostalgia. It has a large portrait of Priya Tendulkar as 'Rajni' (from the Doordarshan TV serial of the same name aired in the mid-1980s) and a blackboard hung on a wall where the menu is written. And waiters wearing white caps. The restaurant had a regular clientele of retired professors, civil servants and defence personnel. And Datta and I, pondering over the latest national and international events, and wondering on which table would women of our age walking in through the door sit.

When I went out for dinner with friends, we would finish it off with a sweet *paan* (a mixture of betel nut, desiccated coconut, sugary balls, sweet preserve, and spices, all wrapped up in a betel leaf). Our favourite stop was a famous paan stall outside the Mehfil restaurant in Sector 17.

A sweet paan tastes delicious if there's sufficient *gulkand* (sweet preserve made from rose petals) in it. There's a technique to eating it. Don't bite the paan immediately. Leave it on one side of the mouth and let the flavours ooze out gently and slowly. I am talking about sweet paan, friends. Tobacco-waale paan is a complete no-no.

I am feeling a bit hungry now. Aren't you?

I know I have not covered loads of incredible, delicious Indian street food here. That probably would need a whole book on its own. May there be one!

12.

Raddhiwaala

I dedicate this chapter to all the '*waalas*' I came across in my life, the traders who made life easier for consumers. *Sabziwaala, dhoodhwaala, paaniwaala, breadwaala, juicewaala,* ice cream waala and the most fascinating of them all, *raddhiwaala.* They have been the untiring foot soldiers of India. What could you call all of them collectively? The term 'hawkers' is used at times. I prefer *roaming traders.*

The raddhiwaala would visit our house every couple of months to collect *raddhi,* our unwanted stuff, and pay us in return. They collected things like paper, glass and plastic. We had a large amount of paper to give away – newspapers, magazines, our old school notebooks, among other things.

Raddhiwaalas carried a manual weighing scale, which mom would scrutinise. We had seen in Doordarshan's afternoon transmission that some unscrupulous traders attached a weight underneath the scale using a magnet to eke out more profit. But you couldn't fool my mom.

Mom also knew what the going rate was per kilo of junk. So, if the raddhiwaala said Rs 4 per kg, mom would counter demand Rs 5. Sometimes the raddhiwaala agreed, sometimes not. More often than not they would meet halfway – at Rs 4.50.

Raddhiwaalas carried the junk on their bicycles, in two large jute bags hanging on either side at the rear. They loaded our stuff into the bags and off they went, leaving us with money earned from junk and, as it turns out, things to write about.

I would wonder what they had done with all the stuff they collected from us. Why did they pay us for getting rid of our rubbish? I reckon they would have sold some of it to *kabaadi* (junk) shops, where it would have been reused.

Recycling waste materials is a welcome habit, practised far more widely these days. It helps the environment. Nowadays, 'upcycling' is also gaining popularity globally. Old or unwanted objects made into new, artistic or designer objects. We can justly say that upcycling had already found its status in India decades ago. In the early 1960s, Nek Chand had started creating objects of art using discarded things, which led to the creation of his now-famous Rock Garden in Chandigarh. I would recommend a visit.

Dhoodhwaala

The milkman visited our house every morning with fresh milk (*dhoodh*) in big metal cans. He poured it in our pan (*pateela*). We used to get 2 litres every day. Unless we had guests coming over or had plans to make *kheer* (rice pudding) that day. There were countless discussions between adults – mom, dad, neighbours, uncles, aunties – on the ratio of water in milk and how dhoodhwaalas diluted milk using water.

Breadwaala

The earliest memory I have of breadwaalas is from the late 1980s. The breadwaala visited our neighbourhood in the early mornings, around 5:30 am. It used to be cold and dark in winters at that time. Final exams in our school wouldn't have been too far away. My sister and I would be preparing for exams in the mornings.

Mom would make us tea, early in the morning or late at night, whenever we needed it, without ever complaining of not getting a good night's sleep. At times she would make *paranthaas*. These were square in shape, sprinkled with salt and *ajwain* (carom seeds or lovage seeds) inside the dough, eaten with butter or *malai* (homemade clotted cream) on top. Or sometimes she gave us bread heated in ghee or butter, sprinkled with some salt.

Now, what better to hear in the morning than the street cry "*taazi* bread" (fresh bread) when you are short of bread. That's what we would hear every morning at 5:30 am, sitting in *rajais* (quilts) on chilly, winter days.

"Taaaazi braiddd." He pronounced bread as 'braid', with elongated 'aid'. The long drawl of 'aid' sounded very natural. He brought bread, eggs and milk – everything you would need for your breakfast – in a small cart (*rehri* in Punjabi) which he used to pedal. I had great respect for that gentleman. He, and perhaps his family, must have got up early at dawn, driven some distance pedalling his cart in cold and foggy mornings and possibly did another job after his morning round.

Paaniwaala

The locality where we lived was farther away from the main town. The houses in the area were newly built and water pipes had not been laid at that time. So, we had to buy *paani* (water).

Water needed for drinking and cooking was bought. For other needs, every house had a motor installed that pumped out groundwater and stored it in a water tank.

The man who brought water, our paaniwaala, was a hardworking man. He supplied water to several houses in the area. He came in evenings pulling several cans in a small cart.

We bought two cans of water twice a week and stored it in a large bucket with a lid.

These were pretty heavy cans, 20 litres each. He used to carry two cans at the same time, one in each hand. I was 15 years of age at that time. I asked him a couple of times if I could help him carry the cans. But he said it was easier for him to carry both cans at the same time as that allowed him to maintain the balance. I could see that it was difficult for him but he ploughed on. Another inspiration for my younger self; another habit for my adult self – not wasting water, at least making an effort not to. Not everyone in the world has it enough.

Sabziwaala

Sabziwaalas brought vegetables and fruits laid out on rehris. Some enterprising ones would shout out names of sabzis – *aaloo*, *gobi*, *gajar* (potatoes, cauliflower, carrots) and the lot followed by a call to buy, "*lai lo*". Some didn't shout out anything but were regular and arrived at the same time every day; so you knew when to expect them. Only immediate supplies were met from them as they tended to be costlier than the market. I suppose they charged a premium for home delivery.

In Chandigarh, the administration had put restrictions on where and when vendors could sell. At times the authorities reached the localities to check if any sabziwaala was trading illegally and would confiscate rehris of those found violating the rules. At that time, the sabziwaalas would just run to save their rehris, leaving an odd piece of aaloo or gobi in the hands of customers.

Juicewaala

When I think of juicewaala the images that flash in my mind are a rehri, a silver-coloured, metallic, hand-operated juicer, a wooden pusher to push oranges into the juicer and a steel pan to collect the juice.

The juicewaala would visit in winter afternoons. My sister and I used to be back from school at that time. We bought juice almost every day. So the juicewaala would stop in front of our house and give a shout (or a '*haak*' in Punjabi). I would take our jug and get it filled with juice. Sometimes the juicewaala's pan already had some juice in it. Mom had taught us to ask the juicewaala not to give us that juice as it would taste sour. Only fresh juice would do.

I used to watch the juicewaala peel oranges (*moussammi*) with his sharp knife, and crush them in the juicer with a wooden pusher while rotating its handle manually. Pulp from the juicer would drop out at the side of the juicer and the orange juice went into the pan. Some juicewaalas also mixed in *anaar* (pomegranate) or beetroot to give the juice a rich, red colour.

In summers, *ganne ka ras* (sugarcane juice) was sought after. Cane sugar was crushed in a mechanical juicer which was affixed on top of rehris. Motorised juicers were introduced later on.

The sugarcane was folded and crushed so many times that the cane turned as thin as paper. Sometimes they also crushed a bit of ginger in it which gave the juice a strong, refreshing flavour. We didn't have sugarcane juice very frequently. It was not considered too healthy, especially because of all the flies buzzing around sugarcane in summers. But make no mistake, chilled sugarcane juice, in hot summer afternoons, was utterly liberating.

Pakorrewaala

"*Har mann pyare Khatri pakorre.*"

This was the placard, written in Punjabi, displayed on the rehri of a famous pakorrewaala during my childhood days in Ferozepur.

The writing on the placard meant 'everyone's favourite *Khatri pakorre*'. But I didn't read it as such back then. The placard fascinated me in more than one way. I had a classmate named Harman. I thought he had something to do with the pakorrewaala. I also knew that my family apparently 'belonged' to the Khatri community. I assumed that the pakorrewaala was from our clan, so must be good.

Perhaps the most common error of mind, they say, is to think that everything that's me and mine is right, the rest is wrong. You could apply this to anything – my car, my child, my habit, my driving, my city, my college, my viewpoint, my country, my faith, my community...

The pakorrewaala's rehri would be stationed next to a busy inner-city road. There was pollution, there was dust, there was cooking oil and lots of it. But people did not seem to mind these things in those days. Mr Khatri did good business. He made samosas and pakorras – gobi, aaloo, onion and *baingan*. Baingan? That is aubergine or eggplant for you.

In Chandigarh, we found a new pakorrewaala. He was a quiet man. His rehri was not next to a busy road, but instead in our local market. He would be at his stand by 4:30 pm and by 6:30 pm his samosas and pakorras were sold out.

His chutney was even more in demand. It was delicious. He gave chutney in small, clear plastic sachets and sealed them by touching them against the hot frying pan. The frying pan not only gave me fresh samosas and pakorras, but also sealed my chutney sachets. Brilliant.

What better day to have hot samosas and pakorras than a rainy day. Which reminds me of a *sher* by Ghalib:

Ghalib chuti sharab par ab bhi kabhi kabhi, peeta hoon roz-e-abr, shab-e-mahtaab mein.

(Ghalib says that although I have stopped drinking alcohol, I have a drink or two when it rains/thunders or during festive days.)

For us, a rainy, cloudy day meant a treat of samosa and pakorra or two, along with sweet *jalebi* and tea. Dad liked tomato ketchup with samosas. He ate ketchup with everything. My sister avoided spicy food and mom was not keen on eating much anyway. So, I had to, reluctantly, for the sake of the good of humanity, eat most of the samosas and pakorras, and chutney and jalebi.

Bartanwaala

At school, we were taught that ancient civilisations did business using the barter system. Money had not been invented. Interestingly, in some places in the world, the system has come back again – people exchanging their skills instead of money. You do gardening for me, I will do plumbing for you. You fix my car, I will give you a guitar lesson. Things like that. In our childhood, we had seen the barter system in action through bartanwaalas.

Bartanwaalas came laden with new *bartans* (utensils) on their rehris and you could buy utensils by exchanging your old clothes. The clothes had to be in good condition though. I used to be fascinated by the exchange. A pair or two of trousers of a growing lad like me would have fetched a small steel bowl or a plate. Not a bad deal. I mean what else could you do with unneeded clothes, if you didn't have a sibling or a cousin or a neighbour who could use them?

My mom, on the other hand, had many tricks up her sleeve, literally. She would rip apart old clothes and make them into bags. Or re-engineer them – trousers became shorts, shirts became handkerchiefs, and so on. And if nothing creative could be done, you could always use old clothes as dusters. But getting new utensils out of them was the most fun. It was like getting presents, and who does not like presents?

Bartan kaliwaala

There was another group of bartan-related tradesmen. When I heard the shouts of "*paahnde kali kara lo*" in our street, I knew it was a chance to see magic. Get your utensils painted or re-shined, literally speaking. These people would re-tin used brass and copper utensils (called *bartan* in Hindi, *paahnde* in Punjabi).

Pots and pans damaged by hearty Indian cooking could be made to look new and fresh in seconds. Non-stick pans were not available in those days and bartans ended up with heavy deposits of oil and food particles. The kaliwaalas carried a small nozzle that emitted some acid which they slowly moved over the inner surface of utensils. It was amazing to watch the sedimented surface being transformed into a shiny, fresh one. The used bartans turned into new in an instant.

Ice cream waala

Ice cream waalas came with their box-shaped rehris. The base of the rehris contained an icebox. It was always a moment of delight when the ice cream waala dropped his hand into the ice cream box and brought our ice cream to life. You could tell how cold the ice cream box was by the amount of vapours emitted from the ice creams as they were fetched from the icebox.

There weren't too many flavours in those days – orange, or the milky one covered in mango, or choco bar. My favourite was milky mango. Some ice creams came in half 'n' half. Top half was usually orange and bottom half milky.

Ice cream waalas attracted children by ringing a metallic bell which was fixed on the top of their rehris with a string attached to it to pull and ring the bell.

Ice cream rehris were visually appealing as well – they were possibly the only rehris to display coloured images in those days. The image was usually of a big orange ice cream on a stick. That level of advertising was enough to make us youngsters drool.

Some other waalas

Then there would be those who gave a shout – "*chaakoo-churriyaan tez kara lo*". They would come around and sharpen your knives. They carried a circular, metallic disc on bicycles. Knives were rubbed against the moving disc, giving a sharp metallic sound and fire sparkles.

Gubbarewaala brought a big cylinder of gas (helium) and blew *gubbare* (balloons). We would gather around just to watch balloons being blown up, hoping that one of them would burst and make a loud bang. Buying them was not always important.

Rugs and carpets were also brought to your doorstep. Most carpetwaalas were from Kashmir, dressed in traditional *phirans* (long, loose coats). They usually came in pairs, which I guess would have made it easier to carry a large number of carpets.

Come to think of all the waalas – you didn't have to leave your house to buy anything!

And finally, some of you might remember watching films using bioscopes. This too was a business. People came around with a bioscope on a bicycle and you could watch short clips by paying 50 paise. We knew the filmwaala was in our street when we heard Bollywood songs being played out aloud. The bioscope had many 'screens – small peepholes, covered by lids and fastened by chains. Now it is the iPhone, WWW and Alexas. So much has changed, so quickly it seems.

13.

Post

$\mathcal{M}$y earliest recollection of anything related to post (or *daak*) is of accompanying dad to the post office to send a telegram (or a *taar* as it was commonly known). I must have been around 6 years old.

The *daak khaana* (post office) was in the same street in Ferozepur as the temple where Bauji (my grandfather) delivered sermons. I have a faint memory of a man sitting behind a counter in the post office, and the tick-tick of the Morse key which he had to send telegrams.

And that's it for the rest of the childhood. I don't seem to have any other post-related memory as a child.

The next thing I remember is getting 'Brilliant Tutorials' in the post when I was studying in class 11 in Chandigarh, around 17 years of age. It was a widespread practice among students preparing for professional exams at the time, mostly under peer pressure, to subscribe to Brilliant Tutorials – learning material covering physics, chemistry, maths, or biology.

The A4-sized tutorials arrived in brown envelopes every month. I opened the first few booklets with interest, read them and tried to process them in my head. After a while, my interest started dwindling. I kept on opening the envelopes but avoided reading the booklets. I suppose this was my way of saying to myself that I am looking at them and keeping them for a thorough read for the next day or the day after or the next week. When my interest nosedived completely, I stopped this formality as well.

How tragic must it be for envelopes that remain unopened. I (my dad, that is) had spent Rs 3,000 on the tutorials. I tried to recover some of the money by trying to sell the booklets. The trouble was that the potential customer I found was related to our family, albeit a far-off relation. That guy was two years junior to me. I said to him that I would give him all the booklets, in perfect condition, for half the market price. That's a good deal, wouldn't you say? I never got to see him again.

All the booklets, some opened, some pristine, were given away to the *raddhiwaala* in the end as junk. My sister kept on taunting me for many years for all the money I had wasted on Brilliant Tutorials, and on all other tuition classes I attended in class 11 and 12, which were commonplace among students preparing for entrance exams. But, then, with the regularity at which the envelopes came in, there was something to look forward to – post addressed to me in our letterbox.

The *daakiya* (postman) visited our locality every day around 4 pm on his bicycle. I would stand on the balcony of our house waiting for the postman to arrive and bring some post for me. Every day I wondered if I would be lucky that day and get some post. You might think how sad it was, but that's because you have no idea how amazing it felt opening an envelope!

The house that we lived in at that time had 3 floors. The landlord's family was on the ground floor, our family on the first floor and another tenant on the second floor. The letterbox, which was on the ground floor, was common to all. I used to be thrilled to see the postman dropping the post in our letterbox.

But the joy was short-lived at times when I did not find any letter addressed to me or anyone in my family.

My visits to post offices became frequent around that time. We wanted to buy a house in Chandigarh. Which meant that our house in Ferozepur would have to be sold. It was an emotional decision for dad. He had got the house built from scratch and had worked hard on it. The land of this house was registered in dad's name on 8 August 1988, or 8.8.88 as he would tell us with delight, for Rs 88,000. Ever since, he has believed 8 to be his lucky number. He was not happy to sell the house, but in the end gave in to the wish of his children.

After selling the house we were expecting to receive its paperwork by registered post. We waited for the letter to arrive for a few days. When it did not, dad asked me to go to the post office to check. I went to the post office and enquired about the letter. I was taken to the sorting room. It was stored with sacks full of envelopes. There were letters and packages everywhere. What a sublime place it was, I thought. So many unopened envelopes waiting to be brought to life. They managed to find our letter and I signed for it.

I would visit the post office, either to buy stamps or postcards or to send registered letters. Most of my registered parcels were for buying prospectus for different entrance exams. The fees that had to be sent along with application forms was mainly in the form of bank drafts, which dad would get made from the bank where he worked. There were times when I had to send money orders, mainly for magazine subscriptions – another chance to visit the post office.

When we are talking about the post, how could I not mention glue. Post offices kept glue (or *goond*) in blue bottles with a stick to apply it. Before glue came into favour, *levi* was used to seal envelopes. It was homemade glue, a thick paste, cream in colour, made of *maida* (refined wheat flour) mixed with hot water. We used levi in childhood for wrapping our books with new covers, every year at the start of a new class at school.

All post offices had a glue bottle. But the bottles were empty most of the time. I hardly ever relied on their glue. I would go well prepared to the post office. Envelopes, Fevistick, cello tape, stapler, paper clips, scissors. I had it all. I took this level of preparedness from dad. He kept all stationery ready. Dad has always been immaculate in his paperwork, earning respect among his colleagues and friends for his planning and attention to detail.

Another splendid habit of dad has been saving money – in bank deposits, public provident fund (PPF) accounts, among others. He had opened a bank and a PPF account in my name as soon as I turned 18. He had also put some money in the National Savings Certificates which were issued by the post office. I would accompany dad to the post office when the certificates were to be renewed or encashed. Not unexpectedly, he kept all the certificates in neat plastic folders (which were then nicely stacked in a tin box he had).

Frequent and regular. That's how I liked my post, in case you haven't gathered that by now. If the frequency dropped lower than my liking, I wrote to random companies or whosoever was sending any free material by post.

Once there was a court battle between the owners of two toothpaste brands – Pepsodent (Hindustan Lever Limited) and Colgate (Colgate-Palmolive) in the late 1990s over the use of *suraksha chakra* (ring of protection) that was shown in Colgate advertisements. The company that won the court case advertised their victory in newspapers and encouraged people to contact them if they wanted to read the full judgment.

"Please write to us at the address given below", they said.

Write I did at the "address given below". Imagine my joy when I received a heavy envelope, A4 in size, with the full judgment and completely unexpected – guess what – free toothpaste. Now that's what you call *sonay pe suhaaga* (icing on the cake).

A postman was an important person and had to be kept happy. We would give our postman sweets during Diwali. It was also expected of you to give some *chai paani* when a postman brought some important documents such as a passport. A small, monetary token of appreciation to the postman. It wasn't possible to get away, especially with passports, as postmen could easily figure out the envelope's contents by its shape and size. The need for chai paani was also felt acutely when police came around for verification as part of your passport application.

With all this affection for the post, it was no surprise that I started collecting stamps. I would remove peculiar-looking stamps from used envelopes and paste them on blank A4 sheets. It was not always possible to remove a stamp without damaging it, so I would cut a piece of the envelope as well. I kept the A4 sheets well-protected in plastic folders. Later, I bought an album designed for collecting stamps and also started buying old stamps from philately shops.

I am certain that it won't come as a surprise that I also collected coins. In fact, coin collection, or numismatics, happened to me before stamp collection. I must have been around 11 years of age when I started collecting coins.

I look back on the first time I paid to collect a coin. A friend of mine at school brought a coin from Tanzania. One of his relatives had returned from Tanzania recently. This was the first foreign coin I had ever seen. I knew I had to get it. There was some negotiation. But considering how bad I am at that, I paid more than the asking price. It cost me Rs 10, a large sum at that time.

Dad's fault. He never restricted us from spending money. We never got any pocket money, he just left cash in a small bag in an almirah at home. If we needed cash, we just helped ourselves. Not that he had a large supply of money, but he made available to us what he had (after saving what he wanted to). This meant we never felt short of money and never felt the urge to overspend or spend irresponsibly.

The coin from Tanzania was a responsible spend, you would agree.

I kept the coins I had collected in plastic sleeves. They were A4-size transparent sleeves. I wanted to keep them in such a way that both the head and tail of each coin were visible. So I would staple the transparent plastic sleeve on all sides of a coin to seal it. This way I created rows and columns of coins, all captured in my staples. Waste of time, you might say. But that, I suppose, was my ikigai at that time.

Talking of coins, I am reminded of a placard that hung in our room when my sister and I were studying in school. She had cut it out from a magazine. It had a quotation, along the lines of: *There are lucky few to get their face on a coin. Most are happy getting their hands on it.*

My fascination with the post continues. Most of it is bills these days.

14.

Doordarshan

The first thing that comes to mind when I think about Doordarshan is its logo rotating on my screen and the well-known tune of the patriotic song *Saare jahan se acha* in the background. It was a good logo. Simple and humble. That is also how the early-1980s were for you.

Doordarshan was established by the government in 1959 as the broadcaster of TV and radio in the country. It will be wrong to call Doordarshan's TV transmission merely a channel, particularly during the 1970s and 1980s. It was the nation's voice, its mirror, and if I am not going too far, its soul. For those who could afford a TV set that is. Or those whose neighbours could.

Some didn't buy a TV set due to high price, some due to fear of the unknown and some were principally against it. But gradually TV picked up and household after household succumbed to its charm, to watch Doordarshan. There was no other channel at that time. Simply Doordarshan.

The earliest memory I have of Doordarshan is dad and Tayaji (dad's elder brother) watching news in the evening. Bauji (grandad) was opposed to watching TV. He hardly ever watched it in his life, except perhaps news at times. As long as we stayed in our joint-family home, TV was watched behind closed doors or when Bauji was not around.

It was the time when television sets were mostly in black and white. Ours was a Weston black and white TV with a blue, detachable screen cover. It had a brown sliding shutter with two doors and stood on four legs.

Hum Log and *Buniyaad* were perhaps the first family soaps on Indian television. I have a faint memory of these serials. Other serials of the 1980s that I can think of are *Nukkad* (with characters named 'guru' and 'khopdi'), *Rajni* (protecting consumers from charlatans), *Yeh Jo Hai Zindagi* (comedy) and *Dil Dariya*, based on the turbulent times in Punjab.

The title song of *Dil Dariya* was profound – *Dil dariya samundro doonge, kaun dilaan diyaan jaane, kaun dilaan diyaan jaane...* (The rivers of heart are deeper than oceans, who can fathom the mysteries of heart?). This song was extracted from a composition by the 17th-century Sufi poet, Sultan Bahu. Shah Rukh Khan acted in this serial, along with other serials in the late 1980s, *Fauji* and *Circus*.

Living close to the Pakistan border in the 1980s meant that we also received PTV (Pakistan TV). Several PTV serials in those days were a must-watch – *Andhera Ujaala*, *Dhoop Kinare* and *Tanhaiyaan*. *Neelaam Ghar*, a game show hosted by Tariq Aziz, was a huge success.

In those days, TV was not a 24-hour thing. There was a morning transmission, an afternoon transmission and news and other programmes in the evening. The news was the mainstay in the evening. We watched news in Punjabi, telecast by the Jalandhar Doordarshan at 6 pm.

News in Hindi from the Delhi Doordarshan was at 8 pm, followed by news in English at 8:30 pm. News was news in those days. No shouting, no glamourising, no inviting 10 people on a panel and giving 5 seconds each to give their opinion on what is supposed to be an informed debate. Newsreaders sat behind a desk, read the news and left. And they were celebrities, a select few, whom the nation heard and saw every day.

Hindi newsreaders on Doordarshan in those days included Salma Sultan, Shammi Narang, Shobhna Jagdish, Sarla Maheshwari and Ved Prakash. English newsreaders included Usha Albuquerque, Rini Simon, Sunit Tandon and Nalin Kohli.

Prannoy Roy started *The World This Week* on Doordarshan in 1988. It was a 30-minute news programme that became a success story and later led to NDTV's 24-hour news channels.

The morning transmission was mainly news, physical workout and breathing exercises. In the late 1980s, Jaspal Bhatti's *Ulta Pulta* became an outstanding feature of the morning transmission. The show had various skits and mini capsules that presented a humorous take on day-to-day life. What fantastic satire it was – socially relevant, punchy and funny.

The morning transmission also had an educational programme by the NCERT (National Council of Educational Research and Training). After that, as far as I can remember, the TV went silent. Wasn't that a delightful thing? No TV for some time.

It came back again at 2 pm, the afternoon transmission. The programmes in the afternoon were targeted at mothers at home and children who would have come back from school at that time. Coming home to chilled sweet *lassi*, delicious food cooked by mom and Doordarshan was bliss.

There was a programme on home remedies in the afternoon. One tip given in the programme has remained with me. When something has gone into one of your eyes and is troubling you, close both the eyes, press a finger lightly against the other eye and rotate it. This will rotate its eyeball, leading to movement in the eyeball of the affected eye, thereby helping to expel whatever was stuck in your eye. It has worked whenever I have needed it.

The afternoon transmission also had *Baingan Raja* – a show where actors came dressed as different fruits and vegetables. It must have been made to inspire children to like fruits and vegetables. Another afternoon programme that comes to mind is *Potli Baba Ki*, featuring short stories narrated by a wise, old man. In the 1990s the afternoon transmission was ruled by soaps like *Shanti*, *Swabhimaan* and *Junoon*. I think Doordarshan wouldn't have advertised any serial as much as *Shanti*. Before the serial was first shown, there were numerous promotions on TV – coming soon *Shanti, Shanti, Shanti*. It certainly made Mandira Bedi a household name.

I liked *Junoon* for the acting of Mangal Dhillon, and Sudhir Dahlvi as Nanaji, and for its title song sung by Vinod Rathod – *na jaane yeh kaisi hai deewangi, keh kaandhe pe laadhe huay zindagi, bhatakta hoon main besabab benishaan, mere saath hai meri awaargi ... Junoon, Junoon, Junoon* (Who knows what is this madness/ obsession that makes me wander around aimlessly, carrying life on my shoulders). Lyrics, music and *mahaul* (ambience, mood) stays with you forever.

Another serial from the afternoon transmission, *Swabhimaan*, churned out several actors who gained success later – Ashutosh Rana, Rohit Roy, Manoj Bajpayee, Kitu Gidwani, Sandhya Mridul, to name a few.

Doordarshan reserved the best for the weekends. And why not. On Sunday morning there was the news, *Rangoli* (a programme on Bollywood songs) and *Gaavo Sachi Bani*, a devotional programme on Gurbani. The *shabad* (sacred song/ word) in the opening title of *Gavo Sachi Bani*, and its rendition (by Bhai Jaswinder Singh Ji, I believe), was captivating:

Koi bole ram ram
Ram, ram, ram,
Koi khudaaye,
Koi … sevay gosaayian
Koi alaahe, alaahe.
Kaaran karan kareem,
Kirpa dhaar rahim rahim.

(In summary, the hymn says that different people call God by different names – Ram, Khuda, Gosayin, Allah, follow different practices, visit different religious places, but there is one cause of all causes, generous and merciful to all.)

Sunday. 9:15 am. All shops shut down. All eyes glued to the telly.

It was now the moment everyone waited for. The moment when the country came to a standstill. It was the time for *Ramayan* (telecast in 1987) and later *Mahabharat* (1988). The epic journeys unfolded on our TV sets.

The actual time of their telecast was 9 am but everyone knew that there would be 15 minutes of advertisements. So people used these 15 minutes to finish whatever they were doing – taking a bath, cooking breakfast, reading the newspaper or getting 'double roti' (what we now call bread) from the market.

For us, Sunday was the day of special breakfast – either *aaloo paranthaa*, or aaloo patties with tomato ketchup, or *aaloo poori*, accompanied by masala chai, made by mom.

Sometimes dad and I would get *poori chhole* or *bhature chhole* from *halwai* (confectionary) shops on Sunday mornings. You were lucky if the queue was short. Everyone seemed to want the same breakfast as us on the same day at the same time. So, if you wanted to avoid the queue you either went early, about

8 am, or late, about 9 am. By 9:15 there was no one left in the market at all.

Many other TV programmes have been made since then on Ramayan and Mahabharat. Granted, the production quality has become better since. The original ones were also shown again during the coronavirus lockdown. But 'that' Mahabharat and Ramayan, on 'that' Doordarshan at 'that' time has no equal.

At 10 am it was the time for programmes for children. There were English fairy tales (Cinderella, Snow White, among others) and the *Guinness Book Of World Records* hosted by David Frost. And cartoons. Over the years a variety of cartoons were shown. *He-Man, Tom and Jerry, Micky Mouse, Mowgli, DuckTales, TaleSpin*, and, I wonder if you remember, *Ghayab Aya*.

Street Hawk and *Knight Rider* also entertained my generation.

Our home-grown private detectives included *Karamchand* (Pankaj Kapoor), *Byomkesh Bakshi* (Rajit Kapur) and Sam D'Silva in *Tehkikaat* (played by Vijay Anand, accompanied by Saurabh Shukla as Gopichand). Not to forget *Raja Aur Rancho* (Ved Thapar).

Professor Yash Pal taught us about science and the universe with his distinctive simplicity and curiosity in *Turning Point*.

Surabhi was perhaps the most admired programme on culture and travel. Renuka Shahane and Siddarth Kak took us to places far and wide in India.

Chitrahaar remained the mainstay of the weekends. There was another countdown programme on Bollywood songs called *Ek Se Badkar Ek* as I grew a bit older.

Param Vir Chakra showed stories of soldiers who had received the Param Vir Chakra, the highest military honour of the country. *Sea Hawks*, starring Milind Soman and Madhavan, showed life in the Indian Navy.

I first watched the programme *Mirza Ghalib* when I was

very young. It did not capture my interest at that time. Many years later my friend Datta gave me a book on Ghalib's poetry. It was written in Punjabi, my mother tongue, which made it easier for me to understand the 19th-century poet who wrote in Urdu and Persian. Datta somehow managed to find out that the author of the book, Mr T. N. Raz, lived in Panchkula (near Chandigarh). He went to the author's house, bought a copy of the book from him and sent it to me.

I started to develop an interest in Ghalib's poetry and bought the CD pack of the TV serial. Naseeruddin Shah played the role of Ghalib and Jagjit Singh sang most of the ghazals in the serial. It was a splendid production, one which makes you think who else but Naseeruddin Shah and who else but Jagjit Singh would have done justice to Ghalib.

Saturday afternoon was the time for a movie. Before VCRs became common, Doordarshan was the main source of movies for most.

Doordarshan was also the main source of coverage for important events such as the Republic Day parade or the Independence Day celebrations. I watched both these events with fondness. I would get up early in the morning to make sure I did not miss the flag hoisting ceremony. Every year it was brought home to us through the familiar voice of Jasdev Singh with his beautiful narration of the two events.

The first cricket world cup held in India was the 1987 Reliance World Cup. This was telecast live by Doordarshan. That ignited my interest in cricket.

I used to be fascinated by *gumshuda ki talash* – missing persons section of the news. People running away willy-nilly from their homes. Handsome rewards were announced at times. Some of the terms used in the show were exquisite, not something we used in everyday life. For instance, *rang kanakbhina* (that is, wheatish in colour) when describing a missing person. The pin code of the Doordarshan Bhawan in New Delhi (110001) was spoken with such beauty in Hindi – *ek ek shunya shunya shunya ek*. I loved listening to 'shunya'.

I enjoyed the animation that Doordarshan used to telecast to spread the message of unity in diversity; apt for a large, diverse nation like India.

Chandaa ek, sooraj ek, taare anek...

(There's one moon, one sun, but multiple stars...)

I also enjoyed watching another melody on the same theme of national unity: *Mile sur mera tumaahra, toh sur bane hamaara.* (Our individual musical notes come together to produce our combined symphony.)

We would wait for New Year's Eve with great excitement. Not that we wanted to go out. Quite the contrary. Our new year routine was that mom would prepare a cake and rice pulao with peas in it. The cake was made in a pressure cooker. There were no ovens at home in those days. And what delicious cake that was. We would gather all the food including *moongfli* (peanuts) and *gur* (jaggery) by 8 pm, sit in bed and switch our TV on.

Doordarshan began the New Year programme after the news telecast, so 9 pm I think. We would have finished eating by then – rice pulao mixed with either homemade curd or butter. Then the new year programmes would start.

There were songs and dance and comedy skits and recap of news and events from the outgoing year. Anupam Kher hosted a new year programme once. He interrupted one of the shows and raised a placard which read – *"Rukaawat ke liye kher hai."* This was a pun on *"Rukaawat ke liye khed hai"* (Sorry for the interruption) – the message that came up on our screens when Doordarshan had technical difficulties.

When the clock struck 12, mom, dad, my sister and I would wish a Happy New Year to each other. There were hugs and there was cake. What a joyful start to the new year.

Doordarshan would telecast English movies on Saturday evenings at 10:30 pm. We watched some of them if mom allowed us to stay awake that late. I can recall watching movies starring Norman Wisdom. I particularly remember watching his movie *Follow a Star* (1959).

Different states in the country had their own transmission on Doordarshan. For Punjab it was Jalandhar Doordarshan. It would telecast Punjabi music and comedy programmes in the evenings, after 7 pm. The music shows were recorded in studios that had simple sets. A mic, a singer and one or two musicians. No glam at all. You would get singers like Gurdas Mann, Hans Raj Hans, Asa Singh Mastana and Surinder Kaur who carried the whole show just on the strength and quality of their voice. No loud music, no digital effects, pure voice.

The comedy skits on Jalandhar Doordarshan were raw Punjabi humour. I probably wouldn't have understood all of them as a child. But now that I recall some scenes, I laugh. So, a man cycling on a village road falls in a shallow ditch filled with muddy water. A man passing by starts laughing. The man standing in the ditch gets upset and lashes out at the passer-by, "*Teri kudi vi taan jagirdaar de munde naal bhajj gayi si*" (Your daughter also eloped with the jagirdaar's [landlord's] son). And that's it. That was the skit. Now, why wouldn't you laugh at that.

Another one – a man asks for a wish and goes to sleep. In his dream, he hears a voice repeatedly "*Ghorra lai ke ayin*" (Bring a horse). He wakes up in the morning and narrates the dream to his friend, who suggests going to a religious place to ward off any evil. Both of them are seen arriving at that place. It's a big building and they enter inside. A booming voice is heard, reverberating from the walls – "*Tenu main keha si ghorra lai ke ayin, tu ghadha lai aayan hain*" (I had asked you to bring a horse; you have brought a donkey, a fool, instead). Told you. Raw humour.

Then, there was this comedy programme in Punjabi where the host asked various questions sent by imaginary viewers, and the expert, Dr Tauliya, would give his *salaah* (advice) to the viewers. A viewer once asked: "I don't know what gift to give as a birthday present."

Dr Tauliya, who kept a hand towel (a *tauliya*) on his shoulder, replied – "*Hawa deo*" (Give them some air). Put some air in an envelope, seal it and present it; it will be good for their health.

I quite enjoyed the programme. It was witty. I once spotted Dr Tauliya at the Khadi Udyog shop in Sector 22 in Chandigarh. The programme did not continue for long, unfortunately.

Several fantasy programmes captivated me over the years. *Stone Boy* was the story of a young boy with magical powers living in Mauritius. *Singhasan Battisi* had 32 magical folk tales. Then were stories of kings and magic in *Vikram aur Betaal*, starring Arun Govil and Sajjan. Some of you might remember its haunting title song – *Vikram, vikram, vikram, betaal, taal, taal. Vikram aur betaaal, vikram aur betaaal …*

We had our own *Star Wars* in *Captain Vyom*. And *Chandrakanta*, a story of a prince and a princess, introduced us to *aiyyaars* (cunning wizards having magical powers).

Neev, a serial that revolved around a boys' school having a strict principal, was an engrossing watch.

Malgudi Days was a classic; so was its title song – *Taa na na Ta na na na na … Taa na na Ta na na na na …*

Then there were comedy serials such as *Dekh Bhai Dekh, Hum Paanch, Shrimaan Shrimati, Office Office* and *Flop Show*. I was fascinated by programmes on Indian history. The best of all was *Bharat Ek Khoj*, based on the book *The Discovery of India* (1946) written by the first Prime Minister of India, Pandit Jawaharlal Nehru, during his time in jail for participating in the Quit India Movement (1942 to 1945). The serial depicted important eras in Indian history, starting from the ancient to the modern era. It was a quality watch.

The title and ending track of the serial were spellbinding and ushered you into the Vedic era. The Sanskrit hymns used in the tracks came from the Vedas, the scriptures that originated in ancient India.

Shall we slide into that era briefly with the title song?

Srishti se pehle sat nahin tha, asat bhi nahin
Antariksh bhi nahin, aakaash bhi nahin tha.
Chhipaa tha kya, kahaan, kisne dhaka tha?
Uss pal to agam, atal jal bhi kahaan tha.

Srishti ka kaun hai karta?
Karta hai vaa akarta?
Oonche aakash mein rehta.
Sadaa adhyaksh bana rehta.
Wohee sach much mein jaanta, yaa nahin bhi jaanta
Hai kisi ko nahin pata,
Nahin pata,
Nahin hai pata, nahin hai pata.

(Before creation there was no truth/existence,
nor untruth/nonexistence,
Neither did space/cosmos exist,

nor did sky or matter.
What was hidden, and where, and who hid/protected it?
At that moment, the incomprehensible
infinite and unrestrainable water too did not exist.

Who is the doer of all creation?
Who maintains the natural order in the universe?
Is that a doer or a non-doer?
Living up there in the sky,
The one who is in charge of everything,
That entity truly knows the truth, or maybe not.
No one knows the answer, no one really knows.)

And the ending song? Happy to oblige.

Woh tha hiranya garbh srishti se pehle vidyamaan.
Wohi to saare bhoot jaat ka swami mahaan.
Jo hai astitvamaan dharti aasmaan dhaaran kar.
Aise kis devta ki upaasana karein hum havi dekar?

Jis ke bal par tejomay hai ambar.
Prithvi hari bhari sthapit sthir.
Swarg aur sooraj bhi sthir.
Aise kis devta ki upaasana karein hum havi dekar?

Garbh mein apne agni dhaaran kar paida kar,
Vyapa tha jal idhar udhar neeche upar,
Jagaa jo devon kaa ekameva pran bankar,
Aise kis devta ki upaasana karein hum havi dekar?

Om, Srishti nirmata, swarg rachaiyta, purvaj rakhsa kar.
Satya dharma paalak atul jal niyamak raksha kar.

Phaili hain dishayein baahu jaisi uski sab mein sab par,
Aise hi devta ki upaasana karein hum havi dekar,
Aise hi devta ki upaasana karein hum havi dekar.

(The one who was the golden womb, established before
creation,
the one who is the lord of all life,
the one whose presence materialises in land and sky.
Which god like that shall we worship by offering our
oblations?

The one who renders the skies luminous with its strength,
the earth green, prosperous, and steady,
and the heavens and the sun steady as well.
Which god like that shall we worship by offering our
oblations?

The one who established fire in its womb to give birth,
and there flowed water everywhere, in all directions,
who arose as the sole breath of life of the gods.
Which god like that shall we worship by offering our
oblations?

O creator of creation, the architect of heavens, our ancestor,
protect us.
O follower of truth and dharma, the incomparable, almighty
regulator, protect us.
The one whose vastness is stretched over all directions,
everywhere, within everyone,
Such is the god whom we should worship by offering our
oblations.)

As is true for all hymns of the Vedas, there is a much deeper interpretation hidden within these words. The literal translation given here wouldn't have revealed the complete meaning of the verses.

Another magnum TV serial on Doordarshan was *The Sword of Tipu Sultan*, which was made by Sanjay Khan. It showed the story of the 18th century ruler Tipu Sultan (played by Sanjay Khan) and his father Hyder Ali (played by Shahbaz Khan).

Chanakya serial was also well-received. It was based on the life of Chanakya (or Kautilya) who lived around 4th-century BC. He was perhaps the first person in the world to write a treatise on politics, diplomacy and the relationship between state and citizen. The serial was directed by Dr Chandraprakash Dwivedi who also played the leading role of Chanakya.

I liked watching budget speeches and parliamentary debates as I grew older. I sat throughout the debate after which the 13-day Atal Behari Vajpayee government resigned in 1996. There were some exquisite speakers in Parliament at that time, including Sushma Swaraj.

The early 1990s brought a flood of cable TV channels in India. Watching TV was never the same. New channels brought variety and choice. But they also brought them in excess. And mom would tell us that "excess of everything is bad". Our family continued to be faithful to Doordarshan for many years.

As I finish this roller coaster journey of Doordarshan, various other programmes are coming to mind. Some of you may also be thinking about other serials which I have missed.

Everything that was telecast on Doordarshan in those days became an intrinsic part of life for us. The only choice you had with Doordarshan was to change the direction of your antennae to get a better signal.

Did you get to move your antennae to improve the signal? Did you shout from rooftops to check quality of picture on your screen? Did you have the pleasure of dozing off listening to white noise when Doordarshan had called it a day?

Those were truly the golden days of Doordarshan.

15.

Advertisements – Test Your Memory

*T*he advertisement industry in India seemed to have realised early on that an advertisement needed to be musical. I can still recall some of the advertisements of yesteryears by their jingles and lyrics. Now, let us see if you can.

There are 40 questions given below based on taglines or jingles of some old ads. Can you identify the brands?

In the questions given below, you will need to either fill in the blanks or guess the brand name. Examples of both types of questions are given below.

Example 1: Sab ki pasand _____ *(answer = Nirma).*
Example 2: Kuch khaas hai hum sabhi mein
(answer = Cadbury's Dairy Milk).

I have not given translations of the taglines and jingles used in this chapter as that would not serve the purpose of the questionnaire. Apologies to those who will not be able to engage with this chapter as a result.

The answers to the questions are given at the end of the chapter. You can score yourself at the end, one mark for every correct answer. OK, off you go.

1. _____ hai jahan, tandrusti hai wahan.
2. Laa, la la la laa, laala laala laa, laa laa laa.
3. _____ nahane ka bada sabun.
4. Tum husn pari, tum jaanejahan, tum sabse haseen, tum sabse jawan ... Saundarya sabun _____.
5. _____ hi lena.
6. Meri twacha se meri umar ka pata hi nahi chalta.
7. Thanda thanda cool cool.
8. Raju, tumahre daant toh motiyon jaise chamak rahe hain.
9. _____, nahi cosmetic, _____ ayurvedic cream.
10. I love you _____.

11. Yeh hi hai right choice baby a-ha.
12. Taste the thunder.
13. _____ the zing thing _____.
14. Lime 'n' lemoni _____.
15. I am a _____ girl. I am a _____ boy.
16. _____ khao khud jaan jao.
17. Mazedaar lazzatdaar swaad swaad mein _____ _____ _____.

18. Ghabraiye nahi, humein kuch nahi chahiye. Hum itna chahte hain ki aap baratiyon ka swagat _____ _____ se kijye.
19. Asli masaale sach sach _____ _____.
20. Namak ho _____ ka _____ namak.

21. Shaadi aur tumse? Kabhi nahi.

22. Zara si hasi dular zara sa.

23. _____ sir.

24. Mann ki shakti, tan ki shakti _____.

25. _____ ki goli lo, khich khich door karo.

26. Fill it, shut it, forget it.

27. Buland Bharat ki buland tasveer _____.

28. Aao chalein hum, lekar apni _____ _____ le, lekar _____ _____ le.

29. Jab main chotta bachha tha, barrhi shararat karta tha, meri chori pakdi jaati... jab roshan hota _____.

30. Yeh _____ ka mazboot jorr hai, tootega nahi.

31. Heera hai sada ke liye.

32. Ispat bhi hum banate hain.

33. _____ ki seeti baji, khushboo hi khushboo udi, mazedaar, lazzedaar khaana hai tayyar, aji khaana hai tayyar.

34. Neighbour's envy, owner's pride.

35. Bhool na jana _____ _____ lana.

36. _____ English-speaking course.

37. Mera waala cream.

38. Jab ghar ki raunak badani ho, deewaaron ko jab sajaana ho, _____ _____.

39. The complete man.

40. Kal bhi aaj bhi aaj bhi kal bhi, in yaadon ka safar toh ruke na kabhi.

How did it go? Remember, give yourself one mark for every correct answer. The scoring key is:

- 0 to 5 marks: you weren't keen on watching TV, were you?
- 6 to 15 marks: it looks like you did watch some TV but were more interested in playing outside (pat yourself on the back if that's the case).
- 16 to 25 marks: were you doing your homework while watching TV?
- 26 to 35 marks: you must be the one who wanted to become an actor/singer/writer.
- 36 to 40 marks: you either have an excellent memory or you did not have much else going on. Either way, well done on scoring this high in the quiz.

Ready for the answers? Please see the next page.

Answers

1.	Lifebuoy	21.	Pan Pasand
2.	Liril soap	22.	Amul butter
3.	OK	23.	Hajmola
4.	Nirma	24.	Bournvita
5.	Fena	25.	Vicks
6.	Santoor soap	26.	Hero Honda motorcyles
7.	Navratna oil		
8.	Dabur lal dant manjan	27.	Hamara Bajaj
		28.	Tobu cycle
9.	Vicco turmeric	29.	Bajaj
10.	Rasna	30.	Fevicol
11.	Lehar Pepsi	31.	De Beers
12.	Thums Up	32.	Tata Steel
13.	Goldspot	33.	Hawkins
14.	Limca	34.	Onida TV
15.	Complan	35.	ECE bulb
16.	Melody	36.	Rapidex
17.	Lijjat Lijjat papad	37.	Asian paints
18.	Pan Parag	38.	Nerolac Nerolac
19.	MDH MDH	39.	Raymond
20.	Tata	40.	VIP luggage

Glossary

Aaloo	Potato
Aaloo poori	Poori (or puri) = fluffy, deep-fried, unleavened bread made of wheat flour, served with potato curry
Achaar	Pickle
Ache bache	A phrase used to mean 'nice children' as opposed to those having bad habits
Ahaata	A stable for horses
Aiyyaars	Cunning wizards having magical powers
Ajwain	Carom seeds or lovage seeds
Akhbaar	Newspaper
Anaar	Pomegranate
Babu	Government officer
Baingan	Aubergine; also known as eggplant or brinjal
Bartan	Utensils (in Hindi)
Basant Panchami	Kite flying festival in the Indian subcontinent to celebrate arrival of the spring season

Basant	Spring season
Bauji	A word of respect addressing one's father or grandfather or any other elderly man in a family; we addressed our dad's father as Bauji.
Bhabhi	Sister-in-law (brother's sister)
Bhagatji	A literal translation of *Bhagat* is a 'devotee'; 'Bhagatji' is normally used as a mark of respect to address someone who is venerated as a religious/spiritual figure (for instance, a guru, a preacher or a priest).
Bhaiya	Brother (usually elder); also used as a word of respect for an elder boy.
Bhature (or bhatura in singular)	Fluffy, deep-fried leavened bread
Bhuaji	Paternal aunt – father's sister
Bhujia	Dry, deep-fried crispy snack, usually made from chickpea flour; similar to what is known as 'Bombay mix' at some places.
Biji	A word of respect used for addressing one's mother or grandmother or any other elderly woman in a family; we addressed our dad's mother as Biji.
Bijli	Electricity

Bindi	Coloured dot worn at the centre of the forehead by women, especially married women, in Indian culture.
Boondi ka prasad	Tiny sweet balls made of gram flour for use as prasad (oblations/offering) in Indian temples
Chaakoo-churriyaan tez kara lo	Get your knives sharpened
Chaat	Spicy mix of fruit or boiled vegetables
Chachaji	Paternal uncle – father's younger brother
Chai paani	Literal translation is 'tea, water'; it is normally used as a way to ask your guests if they would like something to drink or eat. This phrase also indirectly refers to a tiny token of thanks or appreciation (or in some cases bribe) for services rendered, usually by those working in government/administration or public services.
Chakkarvyuh	A military formation containing various layers of defensive walls in the shape of a labyrinth, intended to surround enemies.
Chana daal khichdi	Mix of rice and split chickpea lentils
Chhole	Chickpeas

Chhole bhature	Bhatura = deep-fried, leavened bread served with chickpea curry (chhole)
Daak khaana	Post office
Daak	Post
Daakiya	Postman
Dadaji	Grandfather (paternal)
Dadiji	Grandmother (paternal)
Dahi	Yoghurt; curd
Dahi vada or dahi bhalla	Deep-fried lentil fritters, served with yoghurt.
Dha	See *Sa re ga ma pa dha ni*
Dhanda	Chilled; cold; also a cold drink
Dholki	Also known as dholak; an Indian musical hand drum. It is made of wood and has two heads, one used for bass and one for treble. The heads are made of animal skin.
Dhoodhwaala	A milkman (dhoodh = milk)
Didi	Sister (usually elder); also used as a word of respect for an elder girl.
Doordarshan	Public sector broadcaster (including TV and radio), founded by the Government of India in 1959.
Dora	Line or string used for flying kites; also called manja

Dosa	Thin, savoury pancakes or crepes made with battered rice and lentils; a popular dish from South India.
Ehsaan	Favour
Ek	One
Falooda seviyan	Dessert noodles similar to vermicelli
Gajar	Carrot
Gali	An alleyway or a street
Ghalib	Pen-name of famous Indian poet Mirza Asadullah Baig Khaan, also known as Mirza Ghalib (1797–1869).
Ghee	Clarified butter
Gobi	Cauliflower
Gola	A ball
Golgappa	Small, round, hollow, crispy puff-pastry, often filled with small chunks of boiled potatoes, chickpeas and tamarind chutney, accompanied by spicy water.
Golgappewaalas	Those who sell golgappas
Gubbare	Balloons
Guddi	A kite (in Punjabi)
Gulab jamun	Sweet, fried dough balls, soaked in a rose-flavoured sticky syrup
Gulkand	Sweet preserve made from rose petals

Gurbani	A term referring to compositions (including hymns and poems) of the Sikh gurus and other writers, contained in the Guru Granth Sahib – the most revered scripture in Sikhism.
Haak	A shout; a street call
Halwai	Confectionary/sweet-making shops
Imli	Tamarind
Ji	Pronounced as 'g'; suffix used as a mark of respect when addressing elderly or other venerated individuals.
Job-shob	Used as a slang where the second, rhyming but often meaningless word (here 'shob'), completes the first word (here 'job') to attain a phonetic balance in a sentence.
Jugaad	A frugal innovation, or a hack, for solving problems, often using limited resources
Jalebi	Dessert; sweet, sticky fried batter in the shape of a spiral
Kaju	Cashew nuts
Kali	Paint (used here as re-shined or re-tinned)
Karyana	Independent, family-owned grocery store
Kesar	Saffron
Khadi	Homespun cotton cloth used in India

Kheer	Rice pudding; dessert made with rice, milk, and sugar
Kirtan	Devotional singing, usually in a group
Kishmish	Raisins
Kulche	Soft flatbread, either served with chickpea curry or stuffed with a mixture of chickpeas, boiled potatoes, onions and green chillies.
Kurta	A loose garment like a long collarless shirt
Lai lo	A literal meaning is 'take it' (here used as a call out by street traders to buy their products)
Lassi	A drink made using yoghurt/curd and water; it can be made sweet or salty.
Ma boli	Mother tongue
Maaji	Literal: mother; also used as a mark of respect for elderly women
Maasiji	Aunt – mother's sister
Malai	Cream of milk, usually homemade
Mamaji	Maternal uncle – mother's brother
Masala chai	Spiced tea
Mataji	A word of respect addressing one's mother or grandmother or any other elderly woman in a family; we addressed our mom's mother as Mataji.

Maulabaksh	Literal translation: someone who has been spared (purified or cleared of sins) by one's master or God
Mohalla	A neighbourhood
Munde	Boys
Nanaji	Grandfather (maternal)
Naniji	Grandmother (maternal)
Om tat sat	Sanskrit mantra meaning 'all that is' or the supreme absolute truth
Paahnde	Utensils (in Punjabi)
Paan	A mixture of betel nut, desiccated coconut, sugary balls, sweet preserve and spices, wrapped up in a betel leaf.
Paani	Water
Paani poori	Same as golgappa
Paaniwaala	Someone who sells water (paani = water)
Paapri	Crispy, deep-fried crackers
Paav bhaji	Thick curry (bhaji) made of mashed vegetables served with soft bread rolls (paav)
Padosi	A neighbour
Paise (or singular paisa)	A paisa is 1/100 of an Indian rupee

Pakorra (or pakora)	Deep-fried, battered vegetables such as onions, potatoes, or cauliflower; onion-based pakorras are also known as 'onion bhaji' at some places.
Paranthaas (or parathas)	Unleavened flatbread from the Indian subcontinent, made with wheat flour.
Patang	A kite (in Hindi)
Pateela	A metallic pan used for cooking or holding food or drink
Pecha	Entanglement; also used to denote a battle between kites
Petha	Ash gourd (also called winter melon); sugary, chewy candy made from these is also called petha.
Phiran	A traditional outfit worn in Kashmir; it is a long, loose coat or gown.
Phoren	Hinglish (Hindi + English) pronunciation of foreign
Pitaji	A word of respect used to address one's father or grandfather or any other elderly man in a family; we addressed mom's father as Pitaji.
Poori chhole	Poori (or puri) = fluffy, deep-fried, unleavened bread made of wheat flour, served with chickpeas curry
Pudina	Mint
Qawwali	Devotional music and lyrics practised in Sufi traditions in South Asia

Raddhiwaala	Someone who trades in junk items (raddhi = junk or refuse)
Rehri	A pedal cart used for carrying small loads
Relu katta	Punjabi word used for someone who plays for both the teams in a game
Rooh Afza	A well-known brand of sharbat (or sherbet)
Rs (or singular Re)	Indian rupee
Sa re ga ma pa dha ni	Seven notes used in traditional Indian music (similar to *Do, Re, Mi, Fa, Sol, La, Ti* notes used in Western music)
Sa	See *Sa re ga ma pa dha ni*
Sabziwaala	A greengrocer; a person selling vegetables (sabzi = vegetables)
Salwar kameez	Traditional outfit for women in South Asia
Samosa	Triangle-shaped fried pastry filled traditionally with potatoes, peas and other vegetables
Shabad	Sacred song or word
Shaheed parivar	Martyr's family; shaheed = martyr, parivar = family
Sharbat	Sherbet
Sher	A couplet (in Urdu)

Shunya	Zero
Taazi	Fresh
Tauliya	Towel
Tayaji	Paternal uncle – father's elder brother
Tayiji	Paternal aunt – wife of father's elder brother
Thekedaar	Contractor
Tikki	Fried patty, usually made of aaloo (potatoes)
Verandah	Porch or gallery (open-air or roofed) in a house
Waala	Literally translated as 'associated with'; here used as a suffix to denote a trader or a seller.

Acknowledgements

To my family and friends who became my fellow travellers over the years: I thank you for the journey so far.

My gratitude to those in my social and professional network who gave me encouragement and advice to get my scribblings published.

I would like to thank Jyotirmoy Chaudhuri for editing the book, answering my queries patiently and being a sounding board for ideas.

My thanks to Rupinder Kaur for the illustration at the front cover of the book and to Neena Gupta for the cover design. Thanks also to Ram Das Lal for setting the layout and Manish Purohit at AuthorsUpfront for publishing the book.

About the Author

Vikas Dhawan, 43, was born and brought up in India and has been living in the UK for the past two decades.

He is a leader in the field of data and insights and has worked in various roles in the education sector, including at the UK Civil Service and the University of Cambridge.

He maintains his passion for writing since his teenage years and have been writing for leisure and in a professional capacity.

Music and rhythm are an important part of his life. He enjoys percussion and singing, and admires Sufi and other poetry, folk music and classic Bollywood songs.

He has a soft spot for antiques, clocks and steam trains. He can be found indulging in reading, playing tennis, cooking and walking.

Mom and dad before they got married. Mom was around 18 in this photo, and dad nearly 24. No less than Bollywood stars from the golden days!

Mom, dad, sister, and I in Pahalgam, Jammu & Kashmir. I was around 3 then. I am not wearing the traditional Kashmiri dress as I was not feeling well (that's what I have been told). This trip was our first journey by air.

★ प्रशंसा पत्रम् ★

श्रद्धेय श्री भक्त राम दर्शन जी महोदय

उप प्रधान श्री दिवानन्दा स्टड़ी सर्कल फिरोजपुर शहर ।
पुनीत सेवा में १२-४-७० रविवार को अर्पित किया गया ।

सम्मानाई!

सौभाग्यवती श्लतद् विद्याशा की पवित्र भूमि पञ्चनद के सुदूरवर्तीय सीमा
नगर फिरोजपुर की समस्त जनता को आप स्वहार गर्भित भक्तिरस से पूरित मिले जुले
प्रवचनों द्वारा कृतार्थ कर रहे हो । वह हमारे लिए एक प्रमुल्य विभूति है इसके लिये
हम सब नगर निवासी आपके प्रति कृतज्ञ हैं ।

हे भक्तवर!

बीघब काल से ही आप गीता रामायण तथा जपुजी साहिब सुखमणि साहिब आदि
गुरुबाणियों की तो विशेष रुचि रखते हैं । प्रमाण स्वरूप में गीता के सात सौ मन्त्र
भाव सहित कण्ठस्थ कर रहे हैं । विद्यालय में पढ़ते हुए आपने अपनी प्रद्भुत प्रभा
का जो प्रदर्शन किया वह एक अति श्लाघनीय तथा स्तुल्य कार्य था । आपने निरन्तर
चार वर्ष गीता का गार्मिक प्रवचन किया जिससे नगर निवासी नर नारियों का
जीवन भक्ति मार्ग में प्रसत कराया-निर्धनों की सहायता करने में आप सर्वदा तत्पर
रहते हैं । आपने जपुजी साहिब तथा सुखमणि साहिब के गुढ़ सिद्धान्तों का प्रचार करते
हुए भगवत् भजन आदि को पुष्ट किया । और सिक्ख तथा हिन्दू जनता के मेंभाव
दूर कर रहे हो । आप भिन्न २ स्थानों में मिलट्री पुलिस, बन्दी गृह तथा स्कूल
कालेज और कुष्टाश्रमादि में धार्मिक तथा सदाचार सम्बन्धी प्रवचन द्वारा सुधार
कर रहे हो । आपने अपने जीवन से एक नैतिक सिद्धान्तों को पुष्टकर दिखाया ।

"पूर्वेंवयसि यः श्रान्तः सः श्रान्त इतिमेम्:।
धानुषु क्षीय माणेषु नामः कस्य न जायते ।"

अन्त में हम सब फिरोजपुर निवासी आपके प्रति अति कृतज्ञता प्रकट करते हैं ।
आपने उस नैतिक सिद्धान्त का प्रदर्शन किया जो कि आपके पूज्य गुरुदेव श्री

Prashansa Patram or letter of praise for Bauji (my *dadaji* — dad's father). The letter, which runs into 2 pages written in Hindi, was presented by residents of Ferozepur city (in Punjab) where he lived. Here they offer their praise and thanks to Bauji for illuminating the world around him with knowledge of scriptures, service to one and all and moral principles. 1970. Bauji was around 48 at that time.

Three generations of the Dhawans. Here I am with dad and Bauji at our ancestral house in Ferozepur. I was 27 at that time. Bauji is wearing his traditional white *kurta pajama* and Peshawari turban. People called him Bhagatji with respect. Bhagat Ram Darshan Dhawan (1922–2011). Our beloved Bauji.

ST. JOSEPH'S CONVENT SCHOOL
FEROZEPUR

Name VIKAS DHAWAN .... Session : 1990-91 Class VII-B ....

JEEVAN

Group photo in class 7. I was nearly 13. I am standing in the top row, 4th from left. Our teacher's name was Mrs Chatterjee, if I remember correctly. She was one of the best teachers I've had.

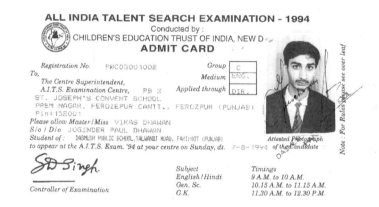

My first passport photo. Aged nearly 16. I was a student of Dasmesh Public School, Faridkot at the time. The signature across my photo is of our Principal, Mr Gurcharan Singh. As coincidence would have it, the test centre for this exam was my previous school, St Joseph's Covent School, Ferozepur. A nice way to end the schooling journey.

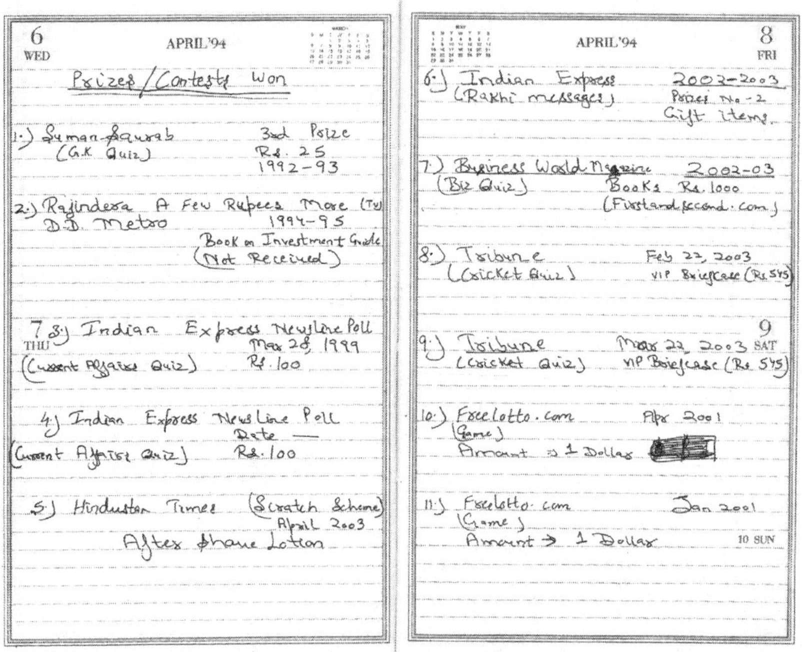
6 WED APRIL'94

Prizes/Contests Won

1.) Suman Saurab (G.K Quiz) 3rd Prize Rs. 25 1992-93

2.) Rajindera A Few Rupees More (TV) D.D. Metro 1994-95 Book on Investment Guide (Not Received)

7 THU

3.) Indian Express Newsline Poll Mar 28, 1999 (Current Affairs Quiz) Rs. 100

4.) Indian Express News Line Poll Date — (Current Affairs Quiz) Rs. 100

5.) Hindustan Times (Scratch Scheme) April 2003 After Shave Lotion

APRIL'94 8 FRI

6.) Indian Express (Rakhi messages) 2002-2003 Prizes No. -2 Gift items.

7.) Business World Magazine (Biz Quiz) 2002-03 Books Rs. 1000 (Firstandsecond.com)

8.) Tribune (Cricket Quiz) Feb 22, 2003 VIP Briefcase (Rs 545)

9 SAT

9.) Tribune (Cricket Quiz) Mar 22, 2003 VIP Briefcase (Rs 545)

10.) Freelotto.com (Game) Apr 2001 Amount ⇒ 1 Dollar [redacted]

11.) Freelotto.com (Game) Jan 2001 Amount ⇒ 1 Dollar

10 SUN

My diary entries of the contests I had won. You might recall my lamentation in the book over not receiving an investment guide I had won in a TV contest. Can you spot my grudge here? The second entry *Rajendra a Few Rupees More* adds 'Not Received'. See, I was not making it all up. It's all there in black and white.

18 Jan 2004

Dear Vijay

Your piece make good reading – lucid & well worded. Why waste arguments on "poor Tesco" & Rushie whole have no rational basis?

I know nothing about internets, E mails etc. I am nearly 90 & don't want to learn.

More power to your pen — the best for 2004 and the years to come

Khushwant Singh

That's the postcard sent to me by the writer Khushwant Singh. 2004. What a delightful moment for me. "More power to your pen", he says at the end.

Printed in Great Britain
by Amazon